# MAXIMUM IMPACT

# MAXIMUM IMPACT

### For Those Who Dream Big and Are Willing To Pay the Price

*Compiled by*
*Tim Storey*

**HARRISON HOUSE**
Tulsa, Oklahoma

*2nd Printing*

*Maximum Impact*
*For Those Who Dream Big and*
*Are Willing To Pay the Price*
ISBN 1-57794-008-3
Revised Edition of previous title, *DARE TO BE BOLD —*
*God Needs Forceful Men*, ISBN 0-89274-557-6
Copyright © 1989, 1997 by Tim Storey

Published by Harrison House, Inc.
P. O. Box 35035
Tulsa, Oklahoma 74153

# CONTENTS

# FOREWORD

by Edwin Louis Cole

Leadership — whether born with a propensity for it, or acquired as a learned ability, always begets influence.

Influence is a commodity squandered by followers, but valued as a treasure and used in great measure by leaders.

In the following pages of this book, you will find leaders giving the wisdom of their life to help us all become better stewards, have finer relationships, and grow in stature as leaders to make the maximum impact possible for God in our lives.

Tim Storey has personally set himself on a course of life to engage and develop relationships with leaders whose influence is not only helping to change lives, but is affecting and changing the world in which we live.

As you read the truths each of these leaders impart to us, it will do the same for you and your world. Thank God for men who are making an impact in the things of God — men willing to invest themselves in God for the good of man, and who are not ashamed to be identified as such.

# INTRODUCTION

*Impacting Men Are Timothys*

*by Tim Storey*

As I sat in my Church History class years ago one cold and rainy morning, I fought to keep my eyes open. The professor was presenting some important but unexciting facts about revival during the past forty years. It wasn't until he started talking about William Branham, Oral Roberts, Aimee Semple McPherson, and Kathryn Kuhlman, that my ears perked up.

As he continued to speak of the great tent crusades in which thousands of salvations and miraculous healings took place, I glanced over at a friend who was a "fellow dreamer." Then he passed me a note that said, "God needs leaders—*be one!*"

As I left the classroom that morning, I decided that I would.... I *would* be a leader for God just like the men and women I had heard about that day in class! My mind teemed with ideas the rest of that day about what I would end up doing as a leader in the Body of Christ. And I began to realize and believe that I actually *could be* a leader in the upcoming revival that God was about to send!

But almost immediately after meditating and thinking those grand ideas, I was forced to examine the realities of my life. My father, an alcoholic most of his life, was killed in a tragic accident when I was only ten years old. And I was reared by my mother, who worked in a doughnut shop.

So here came those thoughts the enemy plants so strategically, "How could I be used in a great way in the ministry when I didn't even have a proper heritage?"

I wanted to be a leader in the coming revival, but I struggled with how could God use me. On and on those fiery darts came, consuming my mind for the rest of that day.

By that evening, I was exhausted from all the thinking and questioning I had done. So I decided to go to my usual "hang out" in the old piano practice room to spend time with God. And when I arrived, I wasn't at all surprised to find my friend John Jacobs already there, because we often met to pray and talk.

When we entered our prayer time that night, John and I knew something was very different. The move of God was very strong and His presence was evident in an unusual way. So John started praying BIG prayers about touching cities for God with a unique tool of evangelism through a special impacting outreach called, the "Power Team." Today, very few haven't heard about the tremendous success John's Power Team has enjoyed in winning thousands to the Lord around the world. In our prayer time, I expressed the same desire to touch cities through signs and wonders.

Well, the Lord must have seen the sincerity of our young, zealous hearts, because He manifested Himself in such a way that would change both of us for the rest of our lives. God's purity and holiness entered the room so powerfully that John jumped to the floor covering his head. So I did the same, figuring that if this six-foot-three, two-hundred-and-seventy-five-pound man was nervous, then I should be too!

Several hours later, when we both pulled ourselves off the floor, we shared and exchanged what John and I came to call "God-ideas."

One of those God-ideas shared with John and I that night was that He would be raising up a new generation of ordinary men, people like us, who would have incredible faith in their extraordinary God. He showed us that He was about to do something great, and that He wanted *every* Christian to be right in the middle of it. So we both accepted God's challenge in the comfort of being reminded that He uses ordinary people to do extraordinary things.

The years have passed since that day in the piano practice room, and God's message has continued to burn in my heart as I have shared it around the world. The Body must become aware of its potential ministries and of the integral part God wants each of us to play in the fulfillment of the Great Commission! (Matt. 28:19,20.)

Today, there are many young Timothys struggling with their part in getting God's job done. Many have received endless hours of book-knowledge, but they lack a modern day Paul to personally mentor and impart God's practical wisdom and understanding to them. And that is why I have compiled this book.

In *Maximum Impact* you will find the wisdom of some of today's true Pauls directed at today's young Timothys for their battles ahead. I invite you to glean from their years of wisdom in areas that range from ministry practicalities, to godly leadership in the home. I have also humbly added my own contribution in the hopes of helping interested readers grow in God's character development process.

To make an impact on anything, we must first be impacted. So it is my fervent desire that *Maximum Impact* will impact you to make the maximum impact possible for God's kingdom today in the world.

# CHECKLIST FOR IMPACTING MEN

Billy Joe Daugherty

1. To do justly.
2. To love mercy, to forgive.
3. To walk uprightly before God.
4. To be poor (humble) in spirit.
5. To have a godly sorrow (to mourn).
6. To remain teachable (meek).
7. To seek righteousness and purity of heart.
8. To be peacemakers.
9. To be ready for persecution.
10. To hate evil.
11. To walk in love with all men.
12. To speak the truth in love.
13. To rejoice.
14. To become a visionary.
15. To rest in the Lord.
16. To maintain the peace of God in your heart.
17. To have faith in God.
18. To be strong.
19. To be instant in season and out.
20. To be bold.
21. To be faithful.

... violent men take it by force.

**Matthew 11:12** NAS

# 1

## *DARE TO BE A LINE CROSSER*

*From childhood, we have been taught to stay within the lines. And we have continued to do this in every area of life, whether denominationally, culturally or racially. Because of that, as a people, we have failed to expand, to grow, to reach new horizons.*

*I believe the Bible is challenging us to be line crossers. We have to cross some lines in order to reach a higher level and to experience all that God desires us to have. It doesn't matter what our background may be, who our parents were, or what color our skin is. God looks beyond all of that.*

*Are you willing to break out of your box to be a line crosser? Are you ready to be an impacting man?*

**Rick Godwin**

1

## *DARE TO BE A LINE CROSSER*

by Rick Godwin

*Pastor, Eagle's Nest Christian Fellowship
San Antonio, Texas*

L et me begin this contribution by sharing portions of an article entitled "Paradigms," written by Joel Barker. I found it a fascinating study.

A paradigm is how we think, how we see things; and people see things differently. We have denominational and religious paradigms. We have cultural, geographic and racial paradigms. A paradigm can be shifted and changed; and we want God's Word to change all of our paradigms so they are right. I know I need adjustments occasionally.

In his article, Barker uses an illustration from life. I will quote briefly from it to stir your thinking.

In 1969, Switzerland dominated the watchmaking industry. They held on to it through most of the twentieth century. At that height of their success they had 65 percent of the world market share in watches and 80 percent of the profit — total market domination. Yet ten years later, their market share plummeted below 10 percent and they had to release fifty thousand of sixty five thousand watch workers.

Can you guess what nation dominates the watch industry today? Japan.

In 1968 Japan had *no* market share. So how could the Swiss, who commanded the watchmaking industry for the majority of the twentieth century and were known for excellence and innovation in their products, be so rapidly destroyed? The answer is a paradigm, a paradigm shift.

Today, many people are wearing that "paradigm shift" on their wrist. It's called the Quartz movement watch. But what's fascinating is who invented it.

The Swiss themselves invented the Quartz watch. But when their research scientists presented it to the watchmakers and to the industry, the Swiss rejected it. It didn't have a mainspring. It didn't have any gears. It couldn't possibly be the watch of the future. In fact, they were so confident it wouldn't be the watch of the future that they didn't patent it or protect the idea.

So the following year, 1969, they presented this watch at the World Congress of Watches. Texas Instruments of America and Seiko of Japan walked by, took one look, and the rest is history.

It's the power of a paradigm. The Swiss were blinded by the success of the old paradigm, and all their investments in it, and when confronted with a profoundly new and different way to continue success in the future, they totally rejected it.

Why? Because it didn't fit into the rules they were already good at following. Barker closes his article by saying this:

"Not even the best watchmakers in the world could stop time. In fact, if you're not careful, **your successful past will block your vision of the future,** which is why we must all develop an **openness** to **new ideas**, a willingness to explore **different ways** of **doing** things. Only through that kind of tolerance can you keep your door open to the future."

Tragically, the Church — denominationally, culturally, racially, regionally — has been the last one to figure out what's going on when something new is coming down the pike.

Now I have no axe to grind and no criticism. I have only a challenge to share with you. Before going to Scripture, let me give you a true-life experience.

I think my preschool teachers really messed me up (maybe you too), even though they didn't mean to do it. When I first began to color, they told me that I had to "stay within the lines." Now there is no such rule in life, but that's what we were taught to do. And it has tended to shrink our thinking and to keep us compacted rather than expanded.

When we as Christians went into adulthood, into marriage, into business, we were thinking, *I have to stay within the lines.* We kept telling ourselves to stay within those lines, whether they were denominational or racial. We just had to stay within the lines! Because of that, as a people, we don't expand or grow or reach new horizons.

I am suggesting to you that the Bible is challenging us to be line crossers.

Now this does not in any way mean we are to cross a line of Scripture. But we have to break out of the boxes of lines that have developed around us — those self-imposed limitations; those cultural and racial limitations put on us, not by God, but by people, by systems, by cultures, by denominations, by religion. I don't ever want to be limited when it isn't God Who limits me!

Kenneth Holderbrand wrote an article called, *The Mundane Man,* in which he says:

"Recently a friend referred to a person as a mundane man. The phrase intrigued me and began to cause me to think. The mundane man, as I view it, is the man who believes only what he sees, only what is immediate, only what he can put his hands on. He might be a truck driver, a banker, a college president, a clerk or a junk dealer. His occupation doesn't really matter.

"The mundane man lacks depth. He lacks vision. The poorest of all men is not a man without money; it's the man without a dream. The mundane man resembles a great ship made for a mighty ocean, trying to navigate on a millpond. He has no far port to reach, no lifting horizon, no precious cargo to carry. His hours are absorbed in routine pettiness. Small wonder if he gets dissatisfied, quarrelsome and fed up. One of life's greatest tragedies is to be a person with a 10 x 12 capacity and a 2 x 4 soul."

Talk about staying in the lines!

God made us for great things, but we will only change in proportion to the people we meet and the places we go. I have never changed by osmosis by saying, "I think I'll just change today." It doesn't happen that way. I was challenged by people I met and by places I went.

Let's say you are pastoring a church in a small-to-medium-sized city somewhere in America. If you thought five hundred was the largest congregation you could have because that was the biggest you had ever seen, then that would be your goal. But if I flew you to South Korea and showed you a church with nearly a million members, do you think you might be expanded by having a bigger worldview, a bigger vision? Your vision would have never been expanded if you didn't go somewhere, see something or meet new people.

This is one of the reasons we must maintain relationships. We have to break out of our little mold, thinking, "Just us four and no more," or wanting to "stay within our little denominational box," both culturally and racially. We can learn something from everybody, even what not to do. We will never change if we just stay in that box and keep hanging around people who say things work only one way.

22

## Dare To Be a Line Crosser

### Cross the Line Like Abraham Did

Consider Abraham. We see him as a visionary, but he wasn't always like that. In the beginning, his name was Abram; he was a heathen, an idol worshiper, a pagan, who lived in Ur of the Chaldees, the southwestern area of what is now Iraq. Abram was nobody until God appeared to him in a wonderful way through grace, and he responded in faith. His name was changed to Abraham, but to fulfill his destiny, he had to cross some lines.

I suggest that you and I have to cross these same lines in order to reach a higher level and to experience all that God desires for our lives. And it doesn't matter what our background may be, who our parents were or what color our skin is. God looks beyond all of that.

### The First Line Abraham Had To Cross:
### *The Line of the Unknown*

If we expect to go where we have never been before and do what we have never done before, then we will be going into some uncharted territory. As I always say, if you want to experience something you've never experienced before, you have to do something you've never done before. If you just keep doing what you're doing now, then nothing will change.

As a pastor, if I want my church to be different and something new to happen, I have to be brave and willing to cross over that line of the unknown. I have to get out there and do something I have never done before.

Now there will be the fear of wondering, *What's out there?* And, *What happens if I fail?* But we have to be willing to step out into deep waters. That's what makes it a challenge. That's also why it isn't too crowded out there.

The problem is, most folks don't fulfill their destiny. They will go to heaven, but while here on earth they live an average life, just getting by.

I didn't come just to fit in. I came to make a statement. I want you to be that way in your life, in your marriage, your ministry, your relationship with God. But you have to cross the line of the unknown by doing something you have never done before. And that involves risk. If failure isn't a possibility, then victory doesn't mean anything.

I want to challenge you with the idea that God has plans for you. Don't be saying, "It's too late for me." You haven't reached retirement as far as God is concerned. It *isn't* too late. It's *never* too late, no matter how old you may be. Remember Sarah. She was ninety years old and still able to have a baby. She crossed the line of the unknown!

**By faith Abraham obeyed when he was called to go out to the place which he would receive as an inheritance. And he went out, not knowing where he was going.**

**Hebrews 11:8 NKJV**

To become a visionary, a person of destiny, you have to cross the line of the unknown. You have to go places you have never been before. You might want to stay in your box and keep doing things the way you have always done them. But there is no paradigm that says you have to keep doing them the same way.

The problem is, to make a change, somebody has to take the first step and cross the line of the unknown. We have to step out into new territory and experience things we have never known.

Most people aren't line crossers because they are afraid of the unknown. Their insecurities rise up and hold them back.

Abraham had to trust God. So, if we expect to go places we have never been and do things we have never done — whether in marriage, in relationships, in ministry, in business, in finances — we will have to trust God like Abraham did.

In my own life, I have learned when you have nothing left but God, you will find out that He is enough. There has been a willingness to step over the line where I have never been before. People who see a better future, a destiny, have always crossed lines and taken risks into the unknown, into uncharted territories. So, I'm willing to cross that line.

When my wife and I were called into the ministry, it was to start a church in San Antonio, Texas. We had never been there. I didn't know how to do it. I had never done it before. I had worked on a church staff, but had never really stepped out like that.

At the time, I had a secure job with a stable income. I was comfortable living in that box. I knew the rules. I knew the boundaries. There was no chance of stepping out of bounds. It was a paradigm.

But God was calling me to another level. When I heard that calling, I received confirmation, so we took steps in that direction — I quit my job, we sold our house, and we headed to San Antonio.

I still remember what it was like to face the unknown. I thought, *But what if nobody comes to our church? How are we going to live?*

Coping with fear of the unknown, I said, "God, are You sure You know what You're doing? I mean, I can really mess this up big time." I remember the lump in my throat. I remember the fears that attacked from the outside, trying to intimidate me by saying, "You'll never make it!"

Eventually, I reached the point where I was just hoping we would be able to pay the rent on the building and have church the next week. Maybe you know what I'm talking about. It would be the same as you having borrowed money to start a business. That was the unknown.

Then I remember facing another *big* unknown for me: stepping into the Charismatic ball game. You see, I was an ordained minister in a major denomination. I was good in my box, and I knew what to do. I knew what was right and what was wrong; what was in order and what was out of order. So I was comfortable in that box. But I became absolutely convinced that there was far more to God than just being saved, and I wanted to go on with God.

I had never been in that Charismatic box, but I had heard some stories about how people acted crazy. I didn't want those demons jumping on me and causing confusion. I wanted to bless people, and I wanted to see the miraculous, but I remember thinking about unknowns, such as speaking in tongues and prophecy. I finally reached the point where I knew I had to take that step and just trust God to help me and to get me to that other level.

Now I am sharing my own life experiences for a reason. I want you to realize that it's impossible for you to grow and to step into a new dimension in any area of your life if you aren't willing to cross the line of the unknown. You can't be murmuring and complaining anymore about your frustrations if you aren't willing to cross that line.

### The Second Line Abraham Had To Cross:
### *The Line of the Impossible*

**By faith Sarah herself also received strength to conceive seed, and she bore a child when she was past the age, because she judged Him faithful who had promised.**

**Therefore from one man** [her husband]**, and him as good as dead, were born as many as the stars of the sky in multitude — innumerable as the sand which is by the seashore.**

**Hebrews 11:11,12** NKJV

Abraham had not only crossed the line of the unknown — he had crossed the line of the impossible. He did things that weren't possible because he had become a person of destiny, of vision. He had become a line crosser!

Charles Haddon Spurgeon once wrote: "God delights in impossibilities. One man says, 'I will do as much as I can.' He says, 'Any fool can do that.' He that believes in Christ Jesus does what he cannot do, attempts the impossible and performs it, for Jesus said, 'If you have faith as a grain of a mustard seed nothing shall be impossible to you.'"

Just imagine what Abraham had to face. He was a hundred years old and his wife was ninety. How could he say it was a vision from God that they have a child at their ages? He had reached a line of the impossible.

As one who didn't come out of the Faith Movement, I have a question for you: "What is the foundation of Christianity?"

It isn't healing or deliverance or prosperity. It isn't feeling good or being slain in the Spirit. All these blessings are part of the package. They can be found in the house, but they aren't the foundation. By reading in Hebrews, you will find that the foundation of Christianity is faith.

You can be a Charismatic and still be in unbelief. Being able to speak in tongues doesn't mean you will have faith. I'm amazed at how unbelieving some believers can be. On the other hand, you can be a member of a denomination and still walk in faith. So, faith is the foundation.

Hebrews 11:6 NKJV says, **But without faith it is impossible to please Him....** This verse is usually translated with the absence of faith, but that is not at all the way it was written. Romans 12:3 says, **...God hath dealt to every man the measure of faith.** So every person, whether saved or lost, has been given a measure of faith from God. That will give you what you need to go to the next level, until you either come into the saving knowledge of Christ or fulfill your destiny by going up the track.

Now we don't all have the same measure of faith, because faith can be built. You can grow from faith to faith. (Romans 1:17.) You can increase strength in that area with victories by believing God. It's like building muscle. So, everybody has some faith.

When God says, "Without faith, it's impossible to please Me," He is talking to the believer and saying: "When you operate in your life, in the level that doesn't require a draw on that measure of faith I gave you, you can have all the religious activity you want, but that still doesn't please Me."

In other words, you are living in that comfort zone, where everything you do is safe. You have reached a plateau. You know exactly what God will do at the level where you are. You don't even need to pray. Life is totally predictable. All your activities are in the guise of Christianity. God is saying, "I love you, but that doesn't please Me."

What a rebuke that would be to me. We should be wanting to check out all the areas of our lives to see if we are stretching.

Now don't be comparing your faith with others. Where you are now should always be a stretch for you. And what seems a stretch for you might not mean a thing to another person. Your actions have to be a stretch on your faith or you won't grow. But even more importantly, if you aren't stretching your faith, God won't be pleased with you.

How sad it would be for God to show up at a Charismatic church and say to its members, "You don't please Me." But that could happen if all of them were doing only what they felt safe with. And they stopped taking risks because of remembering what it used to be like when smacked by that teacher for coloring outside of the lines. They somehow would have had to come to a deceptive conclusion that maybe God is that way. But He isn't like that at all.

We have to believe God for the miraculous. But the non-visionary has never been there, and never will be; he feels that if he hasn't done it, then no one else should do it either. Non-visionary people don't want to believe in the miraculous. But that's what miracles are: clear evidence of God. If we took the supernatural out of the New Testament, we would have nothing. I mean, it's the supernatural life that we are called to live by.

Now I know there are extremes, but I'm not a supporter of all that craziness. I'm into living a supernatural life that's focused on faith. If there is nothing supernatural going on in your life, then take a closer look at God's Word and your life and ask Him for some evidence.

### The Third Line Abraham Had To Cross:
### *The Line of Positive, Instant Feedback*

The moment Abraham crossed that line, he didn't get any positive, instant feedback. And if you dare to cross that line, you won't be getting it either. The only feedback you will get is negative.

Don't be expecting to hear supportive words like, "Attaboy! You're gonna make it! We're with you! We believe in you!" Instead, you will hear words like, "What are you doing, you fool? You're gonna die!" You see, people crouch in fear with negative verbalism.

Hebrews 11:13 NKJV says:

**These all died in faith, not having received the promises, but having seen them afar off were assured of them....**

Abraham worked all of his life for something he never fully received; at least, not in *his* lifetime. But his seed and his seed's seed did. Abraham didn't have the luxury of instant feedback and positive affirmation. He did what he did because it was right, and he kept on doing it because it was right, without having received it all when he died.

Let me tell you this about sacrifice: there is no success without it. If I succeed without sacrifice, it's because someone who went before me made the sacrifice. If I sacrifice and don't see success in my own life, like Abraham, then those who follow me will reap the success of my sacrifice.

You see, as the previous generation for our children, both spiritually and naturally, we should be able to lay down some sacrifices so they can reap the success of it.

Thank God for men like Martin Luther King, Jr., who laid down their lives for a righteous cause. As a result, the next generation has enjoyed privileges and benefits they didn't have to sacrifice for, because other people died for them.

Members of previous generations were treated unrighteously, with gross indiscretion and abuse. If you are enjoying freedom and liberty today, it's because somebody already paid the price.

I want to take my church to a higher level spiritually. And I want to break my kids out of the box I grew up in, because God won't fit in a box. I have to make a sacrifice and lay down my life for something they will see the fruit of. We have to be living for something besides ourselves. Let's live for our next generation.

So when you cross that line, don't expect people to be positive toward you, because there will be lots of negative verbalism. That's why the majority of people aren't line crossers. Most people need to have constant, positive support, being told how well they are doing, or they will be afraid.

You see, there have always been line crossers and pioneers, like the people who led the Reformation. I mean, if they had stayed in their box, we would still be counting beads, burning candles and doing penance. But somebody paid the price and made the sacrifice.

How about you? Are you willing to break out of that box and be a line crosser?

Who will take us further toward racial reconciliation? The blacks alone can't take on the KKK; there must be some God-fearing white believers who will stand with the blacks and help defend them in their struggle. When there is injustice within the black community, they must take a stand for righteousness' sake and say, "We demand the right thing."

If church leaders as a whole in Germany had had the guts to stand up against Hitler, there would never have been horrible places like Auschwitz. But they didn't. Instead, they thought, *I have to protect my good living and my name. It might get uncomfortable to cross that line.* Yes, it might have, and God would have provided for them if they had been willing to look to Him as their Source.

But unfortunately, most people get their affirmation and strength from men rather than from God. That's their security. They think, *I have to be liked and accepted by everybody. I'm terrified to be alone.*

Now you can't pioneer and you can't change if you must always have positive affirmation from other people when God speaks clearly. I would love for folks to like me and to accept what I'm doing for God, but I know I can make it without their affirmation.

There is something else that occurs many times within the black community, just as it does behind denominational lines. For you to do something different, something that hasn't been done within your culture or your denomination, you risk criticism. If a black man succeeds with a multiracial church, then those brothers loyal to African-Americans will call him an Uncle Tom, and pressure will be exerted to pull him back within that box.

Our church is about one-half Hispanic and over one-quarter black. It's multicolored — from the youth to the nursery to the eldership. We represent the culture in which we live.

If you aren't cross-cultural and multiracial, then you aren't American. That *is* America. That's what we are. Without it, we can't grow or have any impact.

But I don't get into the pulpit and preach according to the congregation. I preach the truth of God's Word to human beings who need to hear it. I see it the way God sees it. I don't think color makes a bit of difference in the world. Truth supersedes man's color and culture. If God says it's right, I don't care who I'm preaching to —whether African, Caucasian, Hispanic, Indian, Oriental, or any other racial group. I speak the truth because God said it.

### The Fourth Line Abraham Had To Cross:
### *The Line of the Pull of the World*

Hebrews 11:15 NKJV says:

**And truly if they had called to mind that country from which they had come out, they would have had opportunity to return.**

This verse is talking about God's people who didn't want to return. They desired something better.

You see, the moment you set foot across the line, everybody behind it will do their best to pull you back. Remember, when people won't do what is right, they don't want anyone else doing it either. So the pull of that line will be hardest the moment you step across it because you are still so close to the people behind it, through family ties, long-term friendships, or ministry or business relationships. There will be a tendency to go back, but the longer you stay across that line, the less the pull you will feel on your soul.

Once you step outside your box, you will discover what an incredible world there is out there. You will have reached beyond those boundaries that men have tried to keep you behind — the fear and tradition and lack of knowledge that have kept you behind. Then the joy and thrill of exploration, which comes by realizing what God is doing in your life, will begin to strengthen your soul, and the pull of the world will get weaker.

I don't even think about that anymore, though I thought about it often when I first stepped over the line. Then I began to see God do outstanding things in my life as I partook of the great liberties He provided.

When I realized the incredible blessings I had been missing out on, I got angry, but I wasn't bitter. It was righteous indignation. I felt that I had been robbed of my inheritance as a believer by accepting the limited teachings of my own denomination, sincere though they were. I had been robbed of what God had said was mine, and I wanted to fulfill my destiny.

Remember in Numbers 13 how the Lord sent men from the twelve tribes of Israel to spy out the land of Canaan? Ten of them came back in fear and made everybody else afraid. It took just ten leaders in that "denomination" to keep three million Jews from entering the

Promised Land. Those few persuaded all the others to respond to the pull of the world.

## Stretching Towards Destiny

I must admit there have been a couple of times in ministry when I thought, *I don't want to stretch anymore; I'm stretched out. I'll just coast awhile. I have enough reserves to get by; I could at least bless a few people.* But when that fantasy went through my mind, I quickly rejected it. Had I done that, the moment I stopped stretching and decided to live off my reserves (my past experiences), not only would I have stopped growing, I would also have started to shrink.

There is no stagnation in God's kingdom. We are either growing or shrinking, taking land or losing it.

I have watched as men I started out with shrank back while others went ahead. I too was tempted to turn back, but I kept my face to the wind. I had feelings of pain, betrayal and loneliness. Sometimes the cost seemed just too much. Sometimes I felt self-pity. It was wrong, but it was real, and I have been touched by it all. I finally realized that if I quit stretching, I would stop growing. When a church leader stops learning, the people there won't grow and that church will just wither away.

What we receive by reaching our destiny is not nearly as important as what we become by stretching towards it.

A businessman in his book pointed out the importance of the journey along the way to success. When men get to the top, he wrote, they don't talk about the top, but about how they got there. What makes us what we are, he continued, is our journey — the mountains we have climbed, the slime pit we have crawled out of. All that we have experienced is what makes us great.

The things that cause us pain will become the very things that carry us to our destiny when we respond to them the right way. I'm telling you, every pain I have felt, every bullet I have taken, every setback I have faced, every mountain I have climbed has, when responded to correctly, pushed me towards my destiny.

So God wants us to keep stretching. That's how we reach the destiny He has for our lives.

### What Stepping Across the Line Will Motivate You To Do

**1. Crossing the line will motivate you to trust God.**

Once you step over the line, you have to trust God. Because you won't have any resources to fall back on. You won't even have a map to show you where to go. There is no charted course. Hebrews 11:8 NKJV tells how Abraham trusted God:

**By faith Abraham obeyed when he was called to go out to the place which he would receive as an inheritance. And he went out, not knowing where he was going.**

As long as you stay within the lines, you don't need to trust God. You might talk about it, but you don't do it. You are safe. You know what will happen tomorrow, when to get up, what Bible verses to read and the routine prayer to pray. You don't have to pray about where to go to church or what to do at work; everything is cut and dried.

But once you step across that line, it's sink or swim, live or die. Every moment, you will be conscious of your situation. Nobody will have to tell you to trust God. You will simply pray, "Lord, I've made my decision. Nothing else is backing me up, so I'm trusting You." Have you ever done that? If so, then you know what I mean.

I would like to be what I call a *line pusher*. Then I could be helpful with people who come up to the line in their lives but hesitate. I would sneak up behind them, grab them, and just throw them across that line! I know what will happen once a person gets out of that box: He will expand his thinking and the dimensions of what God has for him. Once he steps across that line, he moves to a new level.

You see, life is either a daring adventure or nothing at all. Once you decide to step over the line, you have to trust God. Just like Abraham did.

2. **Crossing the line will motivate you to sacrifice, to give up today what you can have tomorrow.**

**By faith he** [Abraham] **dwelt in the land of promise as in a foreign country....**

**Hebrews 11:9** NKJV

To follow the vision, Abraham was willing to dwell in an inhospitable wilderness. He sacrificed at first by living in a tent like a Bedouin. But he expected to receive something better down the road. He was willing to give up his comfort for the moment, so that he could fulfill a greater destiny.

The only way we will ever give up our lives and make a sacrifice will be by seeing beyond the present. It has to be bigger than today, or I won't sacrifice for it. If we don't have a vision, we will perish.

It is ridiculous to call on people to sacrifice if we can't give them a vision that is bigger than their sacrifice. Their response would be: "Why should I make that sacrifice and lay down my life? It looks like we lose anyway. I'll just keep what I have. Why be polishing brass on a sinking ship?"

You see, we have to give the Church a vision, a hope of reigning, of success, of destiny, of working today for our children's future tomorrow.

If I have a vision that is generational, beyond me, I will be able to die to my flesh — to temptation, lust, pain — and I will want to have something better than I have now. I will go through it for something bigger than me. I won't be doing it for myself, but for my own children and for their children.

You won't be willing to sacrifice without that kind of vision. But you will be motivated once you cross that line.

**...looking unto Jesus, the author and finisher of our faith, who for the joy that was set before Him endured the cross, despising the shame, and has sat down at the right hand of the throne of God.**

**Hebrews 12:2** NKJV

Sacrifice became a joy to Christ. Not because He was macho and sadistic, but because the Father showed Him a new generation, a new creation. He was to birth what the first Adam had failed at and be the last Adam. God was going to father, or beget, a brand-new generation through the last Adam: the Body of Christ, the Church.

When Jesus saw this in His humanity, He said: "I don't want the pain of being rejected by My Father, but I'm willing to sacrifice for the short term in order to receive the long-term gain."

You must be willing to give up something small today to receive something gigantic tomorrow.

**3. Crossing the line will motivate you to be patient.**

Learning to be patient has been a real chore for me. I don't like to wait. I'm always in a hurry. When we go on vacation, I want to see how fast I can get there. But I'm getting better at it. My wife says I'm growing and maturing and mellowing.

**For he** [Abraham] **waited for the city which has foundations, whose builder and maker is God.**

**Hebrews 11:10** NKJV

A long-range goal will keep you from being frustrated by short-term failures. In almost any endeavor of life, the pathways of success are marked with numerous frustrations, setbacks and failures.

Truitt Cathey is a good example. He started the Chick-Fil-A® restaurant chain. When speaking to a large group of franchise owners, he said: "I know many of you think you've got lots of problems in the restaurant business, so before you tell me your problems, let me tell you mine."

The first hindrance in his life came at birth: he was born tongue-tied. As he grew, he couldn't even say his name in a way people could understand, so he used printed cards to answer their questions.

As an adult, his first restaurant burned to the ground, and his two brothers, who partnered with him in the Chick-Fil-A® business, were killed in a tragic airplane crash.

When he shared his experiences, it was obvious that what he had faced would have made the average man yell, *Uncle!* But it didn't stop him. He ended up building a virtual empire in the South.

Truitt Cathey had, against all odds, made it. He had a dream, and that dream kept him patient. When he got knocked down, he just kept getting back up again. That really encourages me.

So, be patient. Don't quit. Don't give up. When you dare to become a line crosser, when you see something beyond today that God has for you in the future, it will motivate you to be patient.

4. **Crossing the line will motivate you to bless other people, hopefully many.**

   **Therefore from one man, and him as good as dead, were born as many as the stars of the sky in multitude — innumerable as the sand which is by the seashore.**

   **Hebrews 11:12** NKJV

Why was Abraham such a blessing to so many? It wasn't because of the color of his skin or the blood in his veins. He began his life as Abram, a heathen, but then one day he met Almighty God. If Abraham had gone back to living as a pagan in Ur of the Chaldees, then none of us could be blessed today because no nation would have been born from his seed. What made Abraham great was the faith in his heart. He did something no one had ever done before: he stepped across the line.

Are you *wishing* good things would happen to you? Get rid of your wishbone and get some backbone! Step over the line, and some incredible things will happen.

Other men and women in the Bible who were used by God were line crossers. They weren't content just to stay in the box; they were willing to take a risk.

Noah had never seen it rain, but when God said it would, he believed Him. He was willing, against all rejection and mockery, to build a huge boat on dry land and to preach for a hundred and twenty years that God's judgment of man was coming. (Genesis 6.) Noah crossed that line.

Moses had to face a pharaoh who acted like the Saddam Hussein of that day, with control, power, might and military force. But Moses crossed that line when he stood against him and boldly said in the name of the Lord, **Let My people go!** (Exodus 5:1 NKJV). Moses' only backbone came from God!

Esther was an orphan girl, whose parents had died in captivity. A Jew in a pagan country, she lived as a slave. When the king got upset with his queen, he sent his servants to find a replacement, and Esther was chosen. A little nobody suddenly became a princess.

Her uncle, Mordecai, said to her: "God has given you this position for a moment of destiny. By crossing that line, Esther, you can save your nation. You are risking your life to do it, but you have a chance. Who knows — maybe you've come to the Kingdom for such a time as this." (Author's paraphrase, Esther 4:13,14.)

Esther replied: "If I go before the king uninvited to petition for my people, and he doesn't extend the scepter to me, I'm dead. So get everybody to fast and pray for me three days and three nights. If I perish, then I perish, but I'm crossing that line." (Author's paraphrase, Esther 4:16.)

By crossing the line, Esther saved her nation.

Every person God has ever used has said: "I'm not staying like I am, in my comfort box. I'm going to step across the line."

Things won't change until you are willing to do something you have never done before.

5. Crossing the line will motivate you to be persistent, to endure.

**These all died in faith, not having received the promises, but having seen them afar off were assured of them, embraced them and confessed that they were strangers and pilgrims on the earth.**

**Hebrews 11:13** NKJV

God's people spoken of in this verse were confident of the promises, so they embraced them with joy. They just kept on going. Why didn't they quit? Because they could see into the future.

If I can see something in the future for myself, I will keep moving towards it. If God has shown me something, and it hasn't happened yet, then my destiny isn't complete, so I will keep working at it.

We need to be persistent. When we can't see something in the future, it would be easy to quit. But we have to put up with hard times — with abuse, rejection, mistreatment, lack of respect, low pay, obscurity, setbacks, heartbreaks, hurts.

What will keep us going? Being able to see what is ahead. When we haven't made it there yet, we have to be willing to endure. We might want to quit, but if we stop now, we will never get what God intends for us to have.

If I can see what God has in store for my future, and it is better, I won't be set back. I will be persistent and receive what God has promised me.

### 6. Crossing the line will motivate you to maintain your joy.

You won't be happy having to live in small quarters while working a lousy job today if you don't see something better in the future. If there's no faith for the future, there's no power for the present.

What are you hoping and dreaming for? Why not dream big? Dreaming big for the future will give you power for today. But you'll run out of gas fast if you can't see past today.

I remember working on a job unloading freight trucks. I worked for minimum wage, wore greasy overalls and felt like dirt and garbage. I drove a beat-up old car that had over 200,000 miles on it. I had one suit, one shirt, one tie, one pair of shoes, one pair of jeans. My life was easy and stress-free when it came to deciding what I would wear, but I hated it. And I don't ever want to go back to that again.

But I remember my motivation during that entire experience. I thought: *Maybe I'm being mistreated now, being looked down on and given no respect, but it won't always be this way. I know who I am, and my day will come. Things will change. A better future is coming one day.* And I'm pleased to say that things did change in my life!

So, I can remember the way it was, and I will never forget touching the pain, but now I'm looking to go to a new level. I have heard it said, "Every new level — a new devil." And that's true. But if I can't whip the devil at this level, I wouldn't be able to whip him at the next level either. God wants us to whip him right where we are.

## 7. Crossing the line will motivate you to make eternal choices.

Crossing the line motivates me to see more than the present; it helps me to see the future. By seeing the future, I can make eternal choices in my life.

**And truly, if they had been mindful of that country from whence they came out, they might have had opportunity to have returned.**

**Hebrews 11:15**

God's people had a chance to go back, but they chose not to. They wanted something better.

I am living today for what God is going to do in my future. I don't want to live with the regret of not having done more or risked more.

I remember when I was forty-two years old, living in Savannah, Georgia. My life was secure. I made a good income and had a good future. But I was living in a box. That's when I said this to my wife:

"Honey, I know what God is calling me to do, and I'm scared to do it. But something inside me is making me want to do it; I couldn't live with myself if I didn't. If I stay here much longer, I'll be too secure, then I won't ever move. I don't want to live all my life being success-ful here in my little box, wondering, *What if I had done what God told me to do back then? Where would I be now? What would I have experienced? What would God have done for me and through me?* I'll never know these things if I don't cross that line."

I couldn't live successfully in that closed box once I knew God was asking me to do something bigger, of greater risk. I knew I would have to go down before I could go up. I would lose the income, the standard of living, the benefit of ownership I had there in Georgia, and then I knew I might have to sweat it out for years by moving to a hot, dry place like San Antonio, Texas. But I was willing to take that step and move in that direction. It took several years, but now I'm seeing the fruit of my labor.

I'm even beginning to get back to the level where I was when I made the sacrifice to go. And now I have the chance to go to a higher level — and I can smell it. I literally had to go down for years to get reloaded to go higher than I was before. But I will never have to live with the regret of wishing I had risked more or tried more or done something that I knew I should have.

If you aren't willing to cross the line for yourself, then cross it for others. Parents, cross it for your children, for your next generation. You have to cross the line to make your life count.

## Keep Walking by Faith

Do you remember Abraham's discussion with God in Genesis 18 about the destruction of Sodom and Gomorrah? The dialogue went something like this:

"Lord, would You spare Sodom and Gomorrah for fifty people?"

God said, "If I can find that many, then I will spare the city."

"Lord, don't be angry with me; I'm just a man. I know You're holy and righteous and just, and I don't want to test Your patience. But would You spare the city for forty-five?" So God agreed.

Abraham then asked God for forty, thirty, and twenty righteous, then went all the way down to ten. "Lord, would You spare the city for ten righteous?" And each time God said that He would.

Then their discussion stopped.

Do you know why God stopped at ten? Because Abraham stopped at ten. God would have walked as far as Abraham's faith would walk.

Does it look like things have hit a plateau in your life, in your relationship with God, in your marriage, your ministry, or your finances? It doesn't happen to us because God has stopped. It happens because we stop believing God for results.

We are to walk by faith. God says, "How far can it take you? Come on, I'll go with you." Then we will reach a place where it's time for us to cross another line. It could be starting a business or launching a ministry. To reach a new level of income requires some taking and some doing.

My wife and I have always tithed. Early in our Christian lives, we learned about the principles of giving. When we had one daughter in college and another in high school, I remember saying, "Lord, I need something of a new level. I feel like You're making me dissatisfied with the current level, and I have to do something I've never done." So I took our luxury car and sold it. Then I said to my wife, "Honey, don't be embarrassed, but here's a Nissan pickup for us to drive."

Now that wasn't my vision. There wasn't anything about that truck I liked, and I didn't see myself being in it long, but I had to step across a line in sacrifice so God would do something. I gave seed so God could take me to a new level.

Are you willing to cross that line?

My wife and I have made a number of sacrifices that were daring and that really got us into prayer.

Now I'm not telling you about anything that I'm not willing to do myself. I'm simply saying, if we want to see God do something He hasn't done before, we have to be willing to do something we have never done. Let me give you another example from my life.

After twenty-five years of marriage, I noticed that Cindy's and my marriage had gotten a bit professional. We were never unkind or ugly, just cold. As husbands and wives get older, we change; our needs change. What worked well when we were twenty-seven is simply different at fifty-two.

To deal with the problem, Cindy and I joined a marriage counseling class. Six couples met every Friday night for thirteen weeks. In order to "relate," each couple used one workbook together.

To a warrior, a giant killer, nothing is more intimidating and frightening than to be open and exposed to others and to have to "relate." But I realized that my marriage would never be excellent if I wasn't willing to step across the line. I had to do what I didn't want to do, something I had never done.

I felt like I was walking to my execution every Friday night. During those thirteen weeks, I paced in my office all day Friday, knowing "the meeting" was that evening. I was dying inside. I would have rather given my body to be burned. But I knew I had to do it. I went through that door thinking, *Oh, Jesus, help me.*

We went through thirteen weeks of hell, but it changed us. The Word changes warriors, so we both made little changes. I changed some mental attitudes and resentments. Over years of being married, you can let things build up until you don't know why you feel the way you do, but that's a lousy way to have a marriage. We made some choices and some decisions, and it sharpened our marriage and refined us. Now our relationship is stronger and we're best friends.

That experience has been a good example to others. I'm always open with people, sharing my failures along with my successes. That will keep them from feeling second-class because they haven't always been happy with their lives.

You can be a mighty man of God and still be unhappy. You can have a problem in some area and need someone else's help. If you could have helped yourself, you wouldn't have ended up with that problem. That's how it was with me: I needed help from somebody else. So I stepped over that line. It was tough, but the results were wonderful: it produced good fruit. And it was a good example to our children and to our eldership.

There are many paradigm shifts, many lines to cross over and stretching experiences awaiting God's mighty man of faith. For you who will dare to be so bold, adventurous times of new growth and rich blessings are in store for your unusual life. For you who continue to play it safe in the box of the status quo, times of unchallenging religiosity await your predictable, humdrum life.

So dare to be a line crosser. Like Abraham, get out of Ur. Unchartered territories of risk and God's blessing lay before you. Get visionary. Possess your promised land.

## *A WORD FROM GOD*
## *TO HIS FORCEFUL, IMPACTING MEN*

"It is a commandment," saith the Lord.

"From this day on, I have chosen and called you.

"Thou art lifters.

"Thou art warriors.

"Thou art a banner of revival flames upon the cities.

"America *shall* be saved; America *shall* rise.

"Thou art banners.

"Thou art to fan the flames of revival, fan the flames of revival upon a new generation.

"Take revival to a new generation.

"Let your eyes look for new evangelists.

"Let your eyes look for new teachers.

"Let your eyes, this day, choose to walk in the wind of revival.

"Fan the winds of revival; fan the winds of revival.

"Take it to the city; take it to the cities.

"Then fan waves of revival and the flames of revival.

"We are in the latter days, days that men in the past have spoken of, men who accomplished great works in past revivals that swept throughout this nation and unto the uttermost parts of the world.

"The coals lay here this evening.

"Fan them. Fan the fire of revival.

"Commit this day to walk in the flames of revival in your innermost being.

*"Fan the flames of revival."*

# 2

# *SEIZE THE KINGDOM*

*One of the greatest enemies of God's best is something good.*

**– Billy Joe Daugherty**

## *SEIZE THE KINGDOM*

by Billy Joe Daugherty
*Pastor-Founder, Victory Christian Center*
*Tulsa, Oklahoma*

Jesus said that when John the Baptist began to preach the kingdom of heaven was at hand, that people sensitive to what God was saying began to press toward the kingdom, or to move in that direction. They were persistent, determined. They said: "If there *is* a kingdom, if the kingdom of God is coming, we are going to have it. We are going to have all that the kingdom represents. We are going to have the kingdom manifested in our lives. And we are going to take the kingdom fully by force."

**And from the days of John the Baptist until now the kingdom of heaven suffereth violence, and the violent take it by force.**

**Matthew 11:12**

Romans 14:17 says the kingdom is **righteousness, and peace, and joy in the Holy Ghost.** Jesus said, **The kingdom of God is within you** (Luke 17:21).

But think of another way of defining the kingdom. A *kingdom* is where a king rules. Jesus is our King. Wherever the King rules, there will be righteousness. Wherever the King rules, there will be peace. And wherever the King rules, there will be joy in the Holy Spirit.

Where does the King rule? He rules in our hearts.

No wonder Jesus said, **The kingdom of God is not coming with signs to be observed.** (Luke 17:20 NAS.) *It is from our hearts that the King rules.*

So if we are forceful men, who are forcefully taking the kingdom, then what are we after? We are after the rule of the King to be complete in our hearts. If the King does not rule in our hearts, we are not forceful men, and we are not taking the kingdom.

We must be forcefully determining that God's kingdom will rule and reign in our lives. Therefore, the goal for each of us should be not so much outward as inward. What we *are* determines what we do. Our "being" is more important than our doing. Everyone has seen people who become so involved in what they are doing that they forget who they are.

In other words, their actions become more important than their character, and that is the reverse of God's order in His kingdom.

## We Need a Checklist

Our lives are certainly as important as an airplane flight, and each time a plane takes off, the crew has gone through a checklist of things to do. It's particularly important to run through a checklist if you are a young Timothy about to take off in your life and ministry.

Even in a small plane, you need to go through a checklist. If the propeller was not on correctly and flew off about the time you got down the runway, you could be in serious trouble. Or, you might be able to take off without going through a checklist. But what if you hit turbulent conditions? What if you hit a situation that puts pressure on the plane? Suppose you hadn't checked the wings, but there was structural damage, and then the wind hits you unexpectedly?

I remember flying out to Colorado once on a beautiful day. The air was clear and everything seemed fine. Suddenly, we hit an air pocket that threw us up, then down. My two little girls were in the back seat, just bouncing from ceiling to floor yelling, "Whee! Whee!" But I wasn't yelling, "Whee!" I didn't know what was going to happen to that plane!

Do you know that everyone in the ministry can hit turbulent times like that, times that can't be foreseen? So a checklist will help prepare you. You can know your wings are in good shape and can stand that buffeting by the elements.

### Forceful Men Must Do Justly and Love Mercy

The first three items on my checklist of the things God requires of forceful men are found in the book of Micah: to do justly, to love mercy and to walk humbly before God.

God was saying that it is no mystery to know what He requires of us:

**He hath shewed thee, O man, what is good; and what doth the LORD require of thee, but to do justly, and to love mercy, and to walk humbly with thy God?**

**Micah 6:8**

A lot of people love to be merciful. They love to be forgiving, and they show a lot of kindness, but they don't do justly. They don't live an upright life. They are great on mercy and talk about mercy, but *their* mercy has allowed them a licentiousness in their lifestyles. They say, "Well, God forgives; therefore, I can just go do these things."

That is the sort of attitude the apostle Paul was addressing in Romans 6:1,2:

**Shall we continue in sin, that grace may abound? God forbid.**

They are ignoring the first thing mentioned in Micah 6:8: **to do justly**. Licentiousness is not doing justly. We must walk according to the principles and concepts of the Word of God.

Secondly, the prophet said we are **to *love* mercy**. There is a reverse side of licentiousness, a way in which people get out of balance at the other extreme. That is what letter-of-the-law folks do. They are rigid. If you miss a lick in their book, you are going straight to hell, and there is no way out. Those folks concentrate so much on doing justly outwardly, that they miss the mercy, just as the others concentrate on the mercy and forget to do justly.

What does it mean, basically, to be a forceful man? The bottom line is that it means to *be like Jesus*, to be merciful and forgiving. So forceful men are forgivers.

I am forcefully determined that Jesus will rule my life, that I will be conformed to the image of Jesus Christ, that the world will see Jesus in me, and that Jesus alone will be glorified and lifted up.

Jesus was and is a forgiver. He told the woman caught in adultery to **go, and sin no more** (John 8:11). He said to Zacchaeus, "I'm coming home with you; I'm going to your house to eat," and the world of His day looked contemptuously at Him because He ate with sinners. (Luke 19:2-7.) When a woman came and washed Jesus' feet with her tears and dried them with her hair, He let her do it. (Luke 7:37-39.) Blessed are the merciful for they are like Jesus.

There is a real move of God now that is saying to the Body, "It's time to shape up or ship out."

God *is* "jerking out the slack." I believe this is happening, *but* I also know He's doing it in mercy and forgiveness. If you and I need that mercy and forgiveness, how much more do the folks to whom we preach? Am I going to allow them the same mercy that I have needed?

If I say, "No, you are either going to walk the line or get kicked out of the kingdom," I'm not preaching the message of *walking justly before God* in love and mercy.

I have thought about this and know that I have to preach the same thing I need in my life, which is what the Word of God says.

But there are those who are proud of their mercy, and there are those proud to be letter-of-the-law folks. The Lord said through Micah that He does not want us proud of being either one. So the balance in those admonitions of Micah is **to walk humbly.**

### The Forceful Must Learn To Walk Humbly

The Lord said, "Do right. Walk in love. But most of all, *walk humbly* before Me."

I heard someone say one time, "The most subtle pride of all is the pride of grace."

The apostle Paul wrote about this. He said, "Why are you proud or boasting about anything you have? Everything that comes to us is a gift from God." (Ephesians 2:8,9.)

Grace is not of ourselves. That's why we are not to preach ourselves, but Christ.

Some people are proud of how strong they are in faith. Others are proud of how strong they are in mercy. But when you hear their messages, you aren't attracted, but repulsed by the pride that contaminates the Word.

### The Forceful Must Be Humble in Spirit

It isn't enough simply to walk humbly. You must be humble. The New Testament version of Micah 6:8 is Matthew 5:3, where Jesus said:

**Blessed are the poor in spirit: for theirs is the kingdom of heaven.**

So, being humble in spirit is the fourth item on our checklist. Who are the *poor in spirit*? They are the humble people, those who are teachable. We have been taught so much today about the blessings of God and about not being a doormat, or a worm, that sometimes people recoil from that verse. But we shouldn't. Jesus said the *poor in spirit* are blessed. That means they are prosperous, they are benefited, they receive the kingdom.

If you follow the pattern of the Beatitudes in Matthew 5, you will see that this attribute is an entrance into all the others. It is not a mistake or a coincidence that humility is listed first, because only the humble people will enter God's kingdom. Only the humble people will be able to enter into all of the other blessings of the Beatitudes.

**Blessed are the poor in spirit** means, "Blessed are those who aren't arrogant or proud."

Those who are humble are willing to say, "I need help," "I was wrong," "I am grateful."

Proud people don't pray. But those who are *poor in spirit* are willing to admit they need help from God and sometimes from other people.

One day, when I was talking to a man about praying, he said, "I have never had to ask God for anything." This man had never been very blessed either! He hadn't been poor in spirit, and he admitted that he needed God's help.

It takes a revelation on our part to realize that we are not the whole kingdom! We aren't the entire Body of Christ; we are members in particular. The hand can't say to the foot, "I don't need you," and the ear can't say to the eye, "I don't need you."

I need my staff, the people who work with me, and I need the other members of the Body. I have to say, "I need all of you," and if you are humble, so will you.

Sometimes even Christians think it's "macho" to say, "I can do without anybody. I can make it on my own." But God never intended that. He intended for all His children to be linked together by the Holy Spirit.

The third aspect of being *poor in spirit* is being willing to admit when you are wrong. We should all practice this one. If you husbands ever say this to your wives, it will be better than telling her you love her! She will get more excited over it and will say, "Are you kidding? You really admit you were wrong?"

And it hurts to say, "I was wrong."

Admission of mistakes hurts pride. It hurts the flesh. But Colossians 3:5 says to put to death those members in our body that are of the flesh. When you say, "I was wrong," you are laying the axe to the root of pride!

Humble people realize they didn't get anywhere solely through their own efforts. They understand that someone else helped. Think about the people who have helped you get where you are today. You may need to write them a note or give them a phone call.

I grew up watching the Chicago Cubs baseball team and was a particular fan of Ernie Banks. When he signed his first professional contract with the Cubs, he sent a three-word telegram back to his family that said: "We did it."

His father had sacrificed for Ernie to play ball. He had gone to work before dawn and came home after dark so his son could spend time playing baseball. And Ernie never forgot who helped him get to the big leagues.

## The Forceful Are Those Who Mourn

The fifth thing on our checklist is to mourn. What does it mean to mourn? In Matthew 5:4 it means "to mourn for your sins." The sorrow of this world produces death, but godly sorrow works repentance. (2 Corinthians 7:10.)

Those who mourn for their sins are intensely seizing the kingdom, pursuing the rule of the King in their lives. If they sin, it breaks their hearts.

One of the things we see today among many Christians is a lack of mourning over their sins. They are flippant or nonchalant about it. They say, "Oh well, what difference does it make? I blew it; I made a mistake; but God will forgive me," and then just go on sinning. They don't realize the kingdom principle of what happens to their fellowship with God when they violate His laws. The relationship may be intact, but the fellowship is broken.

Another aspect of this godly sorrow is mourning for fallen leaders. Many Christians have felt this in past years about "scandals" in the Church. I personally didn't care to talk about them or to preach about them, and certainly didn't rejoice over them! Others must do what they feel led to do, but I hurt when leaders fall.

Love does not rejoice in evil; love rejoices when truth prevails. Jesus wept over Jerusalem. (Luke 19:41.) Paul mourned over his people and wept in his heart for those who were separated from God and were not coming on into the kingdom. (Romans 9:2,3.)

Those who are going to seize the kingdom will be like Jesus. When they look at a city of people, they will weep over those who need God. The Word says that those who mourn are blessed, for they will be comforted.

Isaiah 61:3 says when we are wounded, the Lord will give us the oil of joy for mourning and the garment of praise for the spirit of heaviness.

### Those Who Take the Kingdom Are Meek

Meekness is another important quality for those intensely pursuing the kingdom in their lives. So, being meek and teachable is the sixth thing on our checklist.

Who are the meek? They are those who are *teachable*. When we are young, vibrant and forceful, sometimes we forget that we still need to be teachable.

The Lord was talking about forceful men when He taught the Beatitudes, because He said the meek **shall inherit the earth** (Matthew 5:5). I am in pursuit of the earth! I am pursuing the rule of God in the earth!

Once when I was in a meeting with missionary-evangelist T. L. Osborn of Tulsa, Oklahoma, Brother Osborn said, "I am still learning. I am still listening. I still want to know more."

All of us younger men are wanting to hear what God has to say! Oral Roberts is the same way. When he lived in Tulsa, he went to different churches, brought his Bible and listened to us younger men preach. A lot of what we preach, we learned from him or others his age. But both Brother Roberts and Brother Osborn are meek, because they are still teachable.

## The Forceful Must Yearn for Righteousness and Have Purity of Heart

The seventh characteristic of forceful men is a quest for being right with God, a quest for the righteousness that comes by faith. They seek the revelation knowledge that through Jesus Christ we have been made righteous. We hunger and thirst for that revelation.

Positionally, through the Crucifixion, we have been made the righteousness of God; but experientially, we hunger and thirst to have every bit of sin removed from our lives in order to be in right fellowship as well as right relationship.

Forceful men are determined to have the same purity on the inside that appears on the outside. Have you thought about the way people see you as compared to the way you know you are on the inside? Forceful men are determined to conquer inner space. America and Russia are trying to conquer outer space. But Christians are to bring into captivity every thought to the obedience of Christ to conquer our inner-space. We are to cast down imaginations, to cleanse our hands, to purify our hearts and to remove the double-mindedness. (2 Corinthians 10:5; James 4:8.)

What does it mean to be pure in heart? It means to have right motives. What are your motives? Why are you doing what you do? What is the purpose behind your actions? Paul wrote to the Christians in Rome that he prayed their love would be sincere. *To be pure in heart is to be sincere.*

Unfortunately, the Body of Christ has lost influence with the world because we have given them reason to question our sincerity. The world began to say, "I don't know if they're real or not. I don't know if they're genuine. I question their motives. I wonder" (to put it in the biblical sense) "if they're pure in heart."

## Blessed Are the Peacemakers

Being a peacemaker is the eighth item on our checklist. *Peacemakers* are willing to wade into broken-down relationships and help resolve the differences. Do people look at you that way? Are you a peacemaker or a troublemaker?

Christians bring a message that cuts through sin like a sword. (Matthew 10:34.) Jesus is a stumbling block to those who will not receive Him. (1 Peter 2:8.) Forceful men want the rule of the King, but they want peace. In order to bring peace, what must be done? A peacemaker must see both sides of the coin and have "the big picture."

Forceful men don't have tunnel vision; they have "eagle vision." They can see that the river changes course a few miles down the road, while others see only what is directly ahead. Forceful men wait on God and soar with eagles. They say, "Hey, down the river a few miles, this thing turns the course."

So it is in relationships with one another. We say there is a point to be won, something to stand up for, yet we follow the apostle Paul, who said to make every effort to be at peace with one another. (Romans 12:18.)

Jesus said, "They will know you are Christians by how you love one another." (John 13:35.)

So, blessed are the peacemakers, for they shall be called children of God. (Matthew 5:9.)

## The Forceful Must Be Ready for Persecution

Number nine on the checklist is to be ready for persecution. We must realize that those determined to obey God at any cost will be persecuted. If we obey God, we are in opposition to the world's system. If we contradict everything the world lives, speaks and thinks, there will be some who will persecute us.

I don't believe the Church is ready for true biblical persecution. I am not talking about being persecuted for our possessions. I am talking about being persecuted for casting out devils and healing the sick.

The first time Oral Roberts began to preach, "Jesus is healing the sick," a guy stood up with a rifle and shot at him. He hit the tent right over Oral's head. That was almost fifty years ago, and the persecution for his teachings hasn't slowed down yet.

Are we ready for that kind of persecution, the kind written about in the Bible?

Biblical persecution is seen in Acts 16:16-24 when Paul cast a familiar spirit out of a young girl, and her owners had him thrown in prison because they had lost their source of income. In 2 Corinthians 11:23-25 Paul talks about having been beaten many times and thrown in prison.

We are not to look for persecution, but we need to be ready to handle it when it comes. Jesus said to rejoice and be glad. (Matthew 5:12.) He was saying, "You are entering into what the prophets got in on, so you can rejoice because you're in good company."

### Forceful Men Hate Evil

The tenth item on our checklist is to hate evil. Proverbs 8:13 says, **The fear of the Lord is to hate evil....**

Why does the author of Proverbs say that? Because if you don't hate evil, you will never avoid it and never get rid of it. There has to be an active attitude toward evil. You can't be passive. Evil comes in attractive packages and is presented in subtle forms. Leaders must have a hatred for evil. They must love sinners, or unbelievers, but they must hate the evil that destroys their lives.

### The Greatest Need Is To Walk in Love

Number eleven is to walk in love. The world and Christians are looking for those who can minister the Word of God — even admonitions — in love. When you preach, people need to know that you aren't mad at the world. Young people are moved by drive and energy, and there is something that drives you on to zealousness — but the greatest need is to walk in love.

**Be ye therefore followers of God, as dear children; And walk in love, as Christ also hath loved us....**

**Ephesians 5:1,2**

We need to preach the Good News and be *glad*, not *mad*. We are not to preach it *sad* or *bad*. The Good News of the Word is always glad. When we preach Christ that way, we are walking in love toward people.

## Speak the Truth in Love

Number twelve on the checklist is to speak the truth in love. In Jesus, both mercy and truth are combined. He is perfectly truthful, yet perfectly merciful, and He has called us to walk in love.

I'm not saying to compromise truth in any way, but at the same time, let's not compromise mercy either. You have to find that place of balance where both mercy and truth are operating. You must be as strong in one as in the other, and you can only do it in Jesus. Only in Him can mercy and truth be preached full strength.

Jesus laid the axe to the root. He nailed the Pharisees, but in the same breath turned around and forgave the sinner. He called them to the plumb line of truth, yet mercy flowed out.

After Peter, one of Jesus' closest associates, had denied Him three times, Jesus said, "Go tell Peter I'll meet him in Galilee." (Mark 16:7.) Peter is what we would call a "real rat." He was an insider who deserted Jesus, who lied and turned his back on Him. How could Jesus be so straight down the line with truth and then turn around and forgive Peter — and us? He could do it because He operates in mercy.

## Don't Exaggerate – Speak The Truth!

Also, I pray that God will deliver us from exaggeration! Let's speak the truth in love. (Ephesians 4:15.) Let's be people of understatement. If you don't know the exact figures, don't stretch them! Whether it's the size of your church, the number of converts, the effect of your ministry or the number of listeners by radio or television — *don't ever exaggerate!* We ruin not only our own credibility, but that of the Church as a whole when we exaggerate. We are better off to simply say, "I don't know."

Why don't we speak the truth? Usually, it's because of some sort of fear or insecurity. We need to remember that the truth will set us free. (John 8:32.) God's Word is truth, and as forceful men, we must speak what the Word says; we must declare the truth.

If someone asks, "How are you doing?" we can speak what circumstances say or what we feel, or we can speak the truth of what God's Word says. It isn't an exaggeration when we speak what the Word says about us. In any area of our lives, when we speak what the Word says, we are speaking truth.

### Rejoice, and Again I Say, Rejoice

The thirteenth item is to rejoice. In Christianity, we have the best thing going. There may be hard times in the world, but Jesus said He had overcome the world. So *rejoice!* Paul was in prison when he wrote to the Philippians, yet he could say:

**Rejoice in the Lord alway: and again I say, Rejoice.**

**Philippians 4:4**

Why could he write that from a prison in Rome?

Why is it true that forceful people rejoice?

Nehemiah 8:10 says **the joy of the Lord is your strength.** Without a rejoicing heart, there will be no strength. Happy people are healthy people. Rejoicing people are strong people. So, rejoice!

### Your Vision Will Make You

Number fourteen is to become a visionary. Forceful men are visionaries. They see visions and are able to envision goals. In Joel 2:28 the Lord said that in the last days He would pour out His Spirit upon *all* flesh. So we will see visions.

Right now, we are rejoicing in what we are experiencing in God. We are rejoicing in what is written in His

Word. We see something beyond what other folks see. We are marching to the beat of a different drummer, the Holy Spirit, a beat the world can't hear. We have a hope out there ahead of us, a motivation that draws us on. Every Christian is a candidate for dreams and visions.

When I was in Oral Roberts University's Christian Education program, we had to do a paper on a model church in one of my classes. The professor said, "Design a church with everything in it that you can imagine, or that you would want."

So I did. I designed a building and wrote down all of the things I could imagine in a ministry. That was in 1974, and in 1984, all of those things were a reality at Victory Christian Center in Tulsa. Every part of my vision had come to pass: the Christian school, the missions training center, the Bible institute, the bookstore and tape outreach, and the television and radio outreaches. All of these areas had been implemented.

Your vision can also come to pass. Do you have your vision written down? Habakkuk 2:2 says to write your vision, to make it plain. Write the goals that are a part of that vision, then begin to write the strategy on how to reach that vision. First of all, of course, seek God on His vision for you. If your own vision for yourself is out of His will, it won't prosper spiritually.

Also, many people have a vision from God but have never asked, "Lord, what is the strategy to reach the vision You have given me?"

Your vision will make you. People with no vision stay where they are. But people with a vision are working on their lives, because they know there are bigger things ahead. They are changing, and their visions are molding and making them. Your vision will determine what is happening in your life.

Do you know the difference between you and people on skid row? The difference is vision. Those people don't have any. They have lost their hopes and their dreams, and nothing is operating any longer to change them.

What's going to take *you* ahead in the race in times to come? Paul said many are in the race but only one wins the prize. (1 Corinthians 9:24.)

Many Christians today seem to think seminars are the answer — and conferences and seminars *are* wonderful. But, if you have no vision, there will be no motivation to act upon what you receive at the meetings. Not everyone can attend a seminar, yet if someone has a great vision, it will come to pass without attending meetings. A person with a great vision will get it on his own. He will study and go after it. He will work, pray and develop himself, because his vision moves him on the inside.

### Forceful Men Rest in God and Live in Peace

One of the biggest challenges to kingdom seizers is how they get any rest. So number fifteen on the checklist is to learn to rest in the Lord. How do you deal with nervous energy? What do you do if you feel that you have to go do something all the time?

Here is a truth that may help you: *Taking the kingdom is not done by activity.* Taking the kingdom comes by obedience, by doing what God tells us to do, by hearing and obeying God.

How can you tell the difference between what is called busywork and being about our Father's business? You will only find that difference when you get into His rest. I'm not talking about lying in a hammock and drinking lemonade. I'm talking about an inner rest, the calm of God, like when Jesus would call His disciples apart from the crowd. (Mark 6:31.) And when He would go off by Himself to rest and pray in order to hear the voice of God clearly.

Remember when Elijah was on the mountain after running from Jezebel, and a great and strong whirlwind came by? Well, God wasn't in the whirlwind. What came next? A raging fire — but God wasn't in the fire. God spoke in a *still, small voice*. (1 Kings 19:11,12.)

Jesus said His yoke is easy, His burden light, and if we come to Him, we will find *rest* for our souls. (Matthew 11:28.) King David knew this when he wrote about the Good Shepherd, Who leads us beside still waters and restores our souls. (Psalm 23.)

*Forceful men are in a position of rest in God.* I have had to learn this personally.

One of our board members said to me one time, "Billy Joe, the problem with you is that you're a race horse." That was years ago, and he was right. If there was something we thought was a good deal, I was on it, just running like crazy to do it. But I thought about that man's statement and decided to make some changes in my lifestyle.

I said, "Lord, I want to give my energy and my time to what will be the most productive."

## One of the Greatest Enemies of God's Best Is Something Good

You can be doing good things and miss God's best. Most people think, *If it's good, I should be doing it.* But is it what God told you to do? You will only know for sure in a state of God's rest.

So number fifteen on the checklist is to rest in the Lord. And item sixteen goes right along with it; it is peace.

## Peace

Number fifteen, rest, and number sixteen, peace, are tied together. In Colossians 3:15 Paul says to let the peace of God rule in our hearts. In Philippians 4:7 he called this the **peace of God, which passeth all understanding.** Isaiah 26:3 says, **Thou wilt keep him in perfect peace, whose mind is stayed on thee: because he trusteth in thee.**

If you don't have peace about something, don't do it. Put it on hold, or don't do it at all. On the other hand, when the peace is there inwardly, and a storm is raging outwardly, you will be able to boldly go through with whatever it is.

You must learn to recognize God's peace.

## Have Faith in God and Be Strong

Number seventeen on the list is to have faith in God. Forceful men are those who *talk* their faith. They speak to their mountains. They declare that every situation will come in line with God's Word. Jesus said in Mark 11:22,23:

**...Have faith in God. For verily I say unto you, That whosoever shall say unto this mountain, Be thou removed, and be thou cast into the sea; and shall not doubt in his heart, but shall believe that those things which he *saith* shall come to pass; he shall have whatsoever he *saith*.**

The tense used here for *saith* is the continual tense. In other words, "Those things which he has said, is saying and keeps on saying will come to pass."

Forceful men are wrapped up in the confession of God's Word. Second Corinthians 4:13 says the spirit of faith is, "I believe, therefore I have spoken." If we believe, we will speak. Believers are speakers; they declare what God has said.

## Be Strong

The eighteenth item God showed me is to be strong. God told Joshua to be strong. (Joshua 1:7.) Paul wrote the Ephesian church, **Finally, my brethren, be strong in the Lord...** (Ephesians 6:10).

If God gives us a command, then He must know the ability to do it is there. How can you be strong? The key to strength in God is your will. You *will* to be strong. I determine that I am strong in the Lord. Joel 3:10 says, **...let the weak say, I am strong.** That is why God told Joshua to be courageous and strong and not be dismayed; He said that no man would be able to stand before him. (Joshua 1:5.)

When we first began to work on getting our building in 1980, three banks were putting the deal together. But after working on it for two months, one of them backed out on the very day we were to close the deal. The man in charge of the negotiations for the bank said, "We're not going to do it. We're not going to work with the rest of them. The whole deal is off."

But God said to Joshua, "No one will be able to stand before you."

So the next day, I called to ask the man if there was anything else we could do or any way we could change things. I got his secretary, and she said, "I'm sorry; he doesn't work here anymore."

I said, "But I just talked to him yesterday afternoon!"

And she replied, "He resigned at 5:00 P.M."

The bank assigned a new officer to work with us, and the whole deal went through. I want to tell you from personal experience that if you will be strong, no man will be able to stand against you. God will move heaven and earth for those who believe in Him.

### Be Instant in Season and Out

John Wesley told his young ministers, "You should be ready to preach or to die at a moment's notice."

Things aren't quite to that point in this country, yet forceful men are to be ready for whatever comes. So item number nineteen on the list is to be instant in and out of season to do God's will. Forceful men are to live on "ready." Punch their buttons, and they will go up. All of us must be ready to meet God at any time.

**I charge thee therefore before God, and the Lord Jesus Christ, who shall judge the quick and the dead at his appearing and his kingdom;**

**Preach the word; be instant in season, out of season; reprove, rebuke, exhort with all longsuffering and doctrine.**

**2 Timothy 4:1,2**

### Be Bold

Item number twenty is to be bold. Proverbs 28:1 says the righteous are bold as lions. Proverbs 29:25 says the fear of man brings a snare; so we aren't to be afraid of men. We must realize that we are to obey God rather than men. We are to respect, honor and reverence men in power and governments. And we are to give honor to whom honor is due, tribute to whom tribute is due (Romans 13:7), *but we also are to realize that God rules over Caesar.* We must please God rather than men.

A bold person is a zealous person. Paul said to be zealous, aflame for God, and fervent in the Spirit.

**Be kindly affectioned one to another with brotherly love; in honour preferring one another;**

**Not slothful in business; fervent in spirit; serving the Lord.**

**Romans 12:10,11**

### Be Faithful

The twenty-first and last characteristic on the list is to be faithful. First Corinthians 4:2 says, **It is required in stewards, that a man be found faithful.** A faithful man will be promoted. If you are faithful over a few things, Jesus will make you ruler over many. When we stand before Him, we want Him to call us "good and faithful servants," don't we? Great ministries are not built in a day or a week. They are built over time by people who are being faithful and doing what God has called them to do, whether or not they are recognized.

We are to listen for God's approval and applause, not mankind's.

There are probably many more things you might want to add to this list. But this one does cover the basics of kingdom seizers.

### Becoming by God's Spirit

You can only become these things I have discussed *by the power of the Holy Spirit.* These things are not burdensome or grievous. The Lord said it was not by might nor by power but by His Spirit. (Zechariah 4:6.)

I believe the Lord has shown you things to add to your list, your life, things that have been forgotten or are new revelations. Just call for God's grace that those things will be added unto you.

If you have been quickened by the Holy Spirit concerning things in your life that you need to repent of or to get rid of, then don't let this moment pass by. Stop reading and go to the Lord in prayer. Ask Him to forgive and cleanse you, to wash you by His Spirit, to create in you a clean heart, to make you a kingdom seizer with a new attitude, right thinking, and humble, forceful motives.

# 3

## *A FIRSTHAND REVELATION*

*A firsthand revelation of God doesn't just impart something to you, <u>it changes you</u>. You become the revelation.*

*I am concerned that much of the Church is like the children of Israel when they said, "We don't want to go up on the mountain and talk to God. Moses, you go talk to Him, and then tell us what He said." (Exodus 20:19.)*

*That was typical of Israel. And isn't it interesting that this attitude is also typical of the Church today?*

*We want to read a book on what the Bible says, instead of reading the Bible. We want to hear a preacher tell us about his revelation, instead of seeking our own revelation from the Word.*

*<u>A secondhand revelation is powerless!</u>*

**— Tommy Barnett**

## A FIRSTHAND REVELATION

by Tommy Barnett
*Pastor, First Assembly of God
Phoenix, Arizona*

Most people are familiar with the story of the woman at the well. (John 4:3-42.) Jesus was traveling with His disciples one day when He said they would return to Galilee by way of Samaria. While passing through Samaria, He waited at a well outside of town while they went in search of food.

Then a woman came to draw water from the well and began to talk with Jesus. She had already had five husbands, and the one she was then living with was not her husband.

Now most of us would have said something dumb to her. We might have said, "You shouldn't have done this."

People come up with the dumbest things to say sometimes.

How often do we wait until something has been done and then say, "You shouldn't have done that"?

Or someone hits you with his car and then says, "Look out!" You wonder if it's because he plans to hit you again.

We seem to operate in our spiritual lives according to our understanding of the Gospel. We seem to focus on the symptom and not the root cause, to speak after the fact and not before.

The woman already *had* those five husbands. So she didn't need a debate about marriage and divorce or a discussion as to which of the husbands she ought to go back to. That wouldn't really solve her problem. The husbands were the symptoms of her problem, not the root — and of course, Jesus knew that.

He went to the heart of things and told her that if she really *knew* the gift of God and Who was speaking to her, she wouldn't be driven by her hunger and thirst for love into seeking another husband or man. She would ask for the Living Water.

If she would take one drink, she would be delivered forever from dependence upon external thrills. That drink of the Living Water would become a well springing up to everlasting life. It would end her futile searching for one relationship after another. It would end her involvement in self-defeating, devastating relationships. She would find fullness and completeness in God.

There is a place God has put in every person's heart, and only He can fulfill and satisfy that place.

Look at John 4:28,29:

**The woman then left her waterpot, and went her way into the city, and *saith to the men,***

**Come, see a man, which told me all things that ever I did: is not this the Christ?**

The Word says that after the woman spoke with Jesus, she went into the city and spoke to the *men*. Those men knew her, perhaps some of them intimately. Maybe some of her five husbands were among those she spoke to about Jesus. This time, however, she was taking a different message to them than before. She was there to proclaim, not to ask. **Come, see a man,** she said to them.

And I'm sure they said, "Uh huh! There she goes again. She'll never change."

But she said, "Come and see this Man. He doesn't know me, yet He told me all about myself."

Then in verse 39, the Word says that many of the Samaritans believed on Jesus *because of the sayings of the woman.*

## Secondhand Revelations Won't Work

That's where many people in the Church are today: They believe in Jesus, because someone else had an encounter with Him and shared his or her experience with them. Perhaps you have investigated and determined that their experiences are true, and on the basis of their testimonies, you established your faith. God help you if anything happens to that person!

Too many people today are satisfied to live in the reality of someone else's experience with Jesus and aren't seeking their own. Now look at verses 40-42:

**So when the Samaritans were come unto him, they besought him that he would tarry with them: and he abode there two days.**

**And many more believed *because of his own word;***

**And said unto the woman, Now we believe, not because of thy saying: *for we have heard him ourselves, and know that this is indeed the Christ, the Saviour of the world.***

There is a point where firsthand revelations become a part of you. Believing becomes a part of the normal Christian life. Let me put it this way: You don't keep talking about something if you have it. Most of us talk about money because we need it and don't have it. If we have enough money, few people — except boasters — will talk about their money.

For example, they say that Rochester, New York, is a city of three thousand millionaires. Some of the richest people in the world live there. Yet a Rolls-Royce agency went broke and had to go out of business. Why? Because Rochester is a city of "old money." People who are used to wealth and have had it for several generations don't usually like conspicuous consumption.

It isn't rich people who talk about money, but poor people — they don't have it. I feel that people who talk about faith all the time are talking to get it, not because they already have it. I'm not critical of that, because the Word says faith is in your mouth. Proverbs 18:21 says the power of life and death is in your tongue. When you speak out, a creative force goes into operation.

However, have you gotten to the point where you can say, "I believe because I have had a personal, firsthand experience with God"? Can you say that you no longer believe because someone else said it, although their experience was genuine? Can you say that you have invited Jesus into your life and your home, that He has answered all of your personal questions? If so, you can say, "I don't just believe on Jesus; I *know* Him."

I am not just going to go cruising through life depending on someone else's experience with God. I determined a long time ago to have a firsthand encounter.

## The Disciples Began Ministering on a Secondhand Experience

This may be difficult at first to see, but the disciples began to move out in ministry on a secondhand revelation. You *can* do a lot of things on belief in what happened to someone else. You can have a lot of things, because someone had a firsthand experience and then imparted it to you. But that isn't the best, and certainly salvation must be a firsthand experience.

Let's take a look at the disciples of Jesus and see the difference in their lives before and after the Crucifixion and Resurrection.

78

## A Firsthand Revelation

While Jesus was ministering, He gave them power and authority over unclean spirits, power to open up blind eyes and deaf ears, power to make the lame to walk and the dumb to talk — even power to raise the dead. They believed because they saw Him doing these things, and they were doing fine until it came to the storm on the Sea of Galilee. (Luke 8:22-25.)

In that storm, why didn't they rise up in faith like Jesus? They couldn't because they had been operating on the basis of what had been imparted to them. Their own faith had not personally been developed, so they couldn't exercise faith over the storm.

*A secondhand revelation is powerless.*

Not long before Jesus ascended, Philip finally asked, "Lord, would You please show us the Father?" Jesus said, "You've already seen the Father. When you see Me, you see Him." (John 14:8-11.) That's when Philip got a firsthand revelation.

Paul wrote to the church at Corinth that they were behind in no gifts, yet they were babies needing milk having no mature knowledge of the Father. (1 Corinthians 3:1,2.) So he sent Timothy to visit them and remind them of the way in Christ.

## What Is the Difference?

When you have a secondhand revelation, you can do some things. But when you have a firsthand revelation, you become the embodiment of that revelation. You have seen it for yourself. That's when the Word becomes life and dwells within you.

In the ninth chapter of John, we read of a man who experienced a miracle from Jesus. He had been blind from his mother's womb and was made to see. Still, he didn't know who Jesus was. So when he was examined by the Pharisees and kicked out of the synagogue, Jesus found him again and asked, "Do you believe on the Son of God?" to which he replied, "Tell me who He is that I might believe on Him." (vv. 35,36.)

So, as you see, you can experience miracles and still lack a firsthand encounter with God. That man had met Jesus and been healed by Him, but he didn't have a firsthand revelation that Jesus was the Son of God. But after Jesus revealed Himself to him, the man said, **Lord, I believe. And he worshipped him** (John 9:38). Then he had a firsthand revelation.

When you receive a firsthand revelation, you don't talk in the second and third person. When you have an encounter with God, it's like Moses when he came down from Mount Sinai. The people looked at his face and said, "Oh yes, he's been talking with God."

There are those who *have* the gift of faith, and those who talk about faith. There are those who have the gift of healing, and there are those who follow them and live on the experiences of the ones with the gift. There must be a transition for those who follow when they no longer believe because of what their mother or father said, or because of what their favorite evangelist or pastor said. There comes a time when we all must stand on our own revelation.

I was reared in a minister's home, so I worry somewhat about those who come out of Christian homes with secondhand and thirdhand experiences. It's possible to take on spiritual things as you take on cultural influences, as a learned, but not an experienced thing. You can get so used to the things of God that you forget to fear His wrath and even take His goodness for granted.

### Don't Take on Someone Else's Experience

When I was in high school, I began to have sincere doubts about my salvation: *Was the Bible really true?*

## A Firsthand Revelation

*Was there a hell? Was there a heaven?* So I decided to read the Bible from cover to cover and not use any kind of helps, then just ask God for myself, "Is there a God? Is this Your Word? Are these things true?" And I told myself that when I finished reading God's Word, if I had any doubts, that I would just put it aside.

But, as I continued to read, I saw things predicted in the Old Testament, like television, the automobile, even the telephone. I began to burn inside as I read the Word and saw things coming to pass. Soon, I said, "It's real!" The Word became a firsthand revelation to me.

Abraham's experience became Isaac's, and Isaac's became Jacob's. They talked of the "God of their fathers," yet each needed a personal encounter with God. Though they were inheritors of the covenant, they each had to have a personal relationship with their covenant God. Their fathers' relationships weren't enough.

All of us know the covenant is for us today, but do we really know this in a personal way?

In Genesis 32 when an angel met Jacob on the way back from his Uncle Laban's to his father's home, he wrestled with Jacob until the break of day. Then the angel asked him, "What's your name?" (v. 27.) That always struck me as kind of strange — even funny. Surely the angel knew what Jacob's name was! I now realize that the Lord was really asking Jacob, through the angel, to own up to what he was. God was saying, "You're a supplanter, a deceiver, a trickster, Jacob. Own up to it. You're in the covenant by birthright, by My purpose. But you're seeking to gain these things by way of yourself, not Me."

When Jacob saw this and admitted who he was, the presence of God came upon him. Then God said to him, "You are no longer Jacob; you are now Israel." (v. 28.)

Jacob had been blessed in a tremendous way. A firsthand revelation of God doesn't just impart something to you, it *changes* you. You, as Jacob experienced, become the revelation.

I'm concerned that much of the Church today is like the children of Israel were when they said: "We don't want to go up on the mountain and talk to God. We'll let Moses talk to Him and then tell us what He said." That was typical of Israel, just as it is typical of much of the church.

We want to read a book on what the Bible says, instead of reading the Bible. We want to hear a preacher tell us about his revelation, instead of seeking our own revelation from the Word.

Jesus pointed out to the Jews of His day that many living in Israel were hungry in the time of famine during Elijah's ministry (1 Kings 17, 18), yet the prophet had to go to Zarephath to find a widow who was ready for a firsthand revelation. (Luke 4:25,26.) Jesus said there were many lepers in Israel, yet Naaman from Syria was the one to receive the miracle. (Luke 4:27.)

Isn't it interesting that outsiders to the covenant seemed to show the most faith even in Jesus' time. The Syrophenician woman had no right to the "children's bread," yet she persisted in order to get her daughter healed. (Mark 7:24-30.)

Jesus, speaking of the centurion whose servant He had healed, said, "I have not seen this kind of faith in all of Israel." (Luke 7:9.)

Even today, it seems that new converts have more faith than those who have been raised in church. The greater faith doesn't ask God to give us things, it claims our entire inheritance. The Bible says we are heirs of God and joint-heirs with Jesus. (Romans 8:17.) When you have a firsthand revelation of God, you no longer have to ride on someone else's experience. A firsthand revelation is your right under the covenant.

You can say in the middle of changing times, "I know Whom I believe." (2 Timothy 1:12.)

## Don't Pattern Your Ministry After Others

I certainly believe in church growth. I travel and speak in a lot of places challenging pastors to build churches and win souls, to find a need and meet it or to find a hurt and heal it. But I believe a lot of people are building churches on secondhand revelations.

If everyone else is doing it, we tend to think it's God. We think every church must have a television program, a school, or whatever the others have. But, secondhand revelation is nothing more than a copy of other people's firsthand revelations.

So I am saying to those pastors: "Go to the mountain yourself. Find out what God is saying to *you*. Get the pattern for your ministry from God. Whatever you do, stick with your own gift, ability and unique calling."

The hardest thing for me to get pastors and laymen to admit is that they never asked God in the first place!

Most people feel, "Why ask Him? If everyone else is doing it, how can it not be God?"

So let me strongly urge you, as a forceful man of God, not to settle for someone else's personal experience. Get your own.

For years after Dr. David Yonggi Cho developed his prayer-cell ministry, people all over America jumped on the bandwagon. And today, most of them no longer have cell groups. Why? They said that if it worked for Dr. Cho, it would work for them — but it didn't. I never got on that bandwagon, because I had no firsthand revelation of prayer-cell groups for my church. I believe that for America, the plan must be a little different. We are a different society with different cultural and traditional habits and patterns.

## Jesus Drives Out Thieves and Robbers

You ought to pause right here and seek God for a first-hand revelation. Let me warn you that when you do, He will get into your life, into your love life, into your relationships. Like the woman at the well, He will talk to you about how many "husbands" you have.

I'm afraid we always read the account of how Jesus drove the moneychangers out of the temple in a literal way and miss the spiritual application. Did you know that you are the temple of God if you have been born again? Well, did you also know that although you have been saved and filled with the Holy Spirit, you still have "thieves and robbers" in the temple?

Negative thoughts and self-images, the spirit of condemnation, the burden of guilt, the fear of failure, the inability to accept success if it comes to you — all of these things, and more, are "thieves and robbers," money-changers who change the coin of your spiritual inheritance into other coins.

When Jesus comes into your life, He drives out thieves and robbers that destroy the realization of the fulfillment of all the promises God has given you. You have to receive these promises as firsthand revelation. At the same time, you can expect persecution from some of those who don't yet have such revelations.

I decided that I wanted God to bless me, and I know what it takes. I want to be near Him, and I know how to get near Him. I have learned to go where He is. The Word says that if we will draw near to Him, He will draw near to us. (James 4:8.) But it also says we are not to forsake assembling together, for where two or three of us are gathered, He will be in our midst. (Hebrews 10:25; Matthew 18:20.) I want God to bless me.

Suppose the Samaritans had said of the woman's words: "Here is a woman whose past we know well. And look how she has changed! Do you see the tremendous change? Listen to her great testimony of her revelation of the Son of God! Come on let's build a shrine for her right here." Don't you settle for that! Don't look to others for your revelation of Christ.

Many churches have settled for old revelations from their pastors or denominational leaders for years. When you go visit, all you hear is the pastor's vision. Don't settle for that. As a people with firsthand rights, don't settle for secondhand revelations.

There is an intellectual understanding of the Gospel, and there is an experience of the Gospel where the light of Jesus Christ comes shining right into your heart. When the Gospel shines into your heart, you are never the same.

Some preachers seemed to have such an effective ministry, yet they fell. The reason they fell is that many of them were cruising along on secondhand revelations. Someone with a firsthand revelation was able to communicate and impart to them their truths. They were able to do much on that impartation, but in the long run, it wasn't enough.

I'm not against following others as they follow the Lord. Paul said that was a valid walk. (2 Thessalonians 3:7-9.) However, it can't stop there. Once you have gone up to the mountain yourself, something in you dies forever. No man can see God and live in the old nature. Because when you see God, something in you dies and something else comes alive forever in its place — a new nature that is in the image of Christ.

When Isaiah saw the Lord, he said, **Woe is me! for I am undone...** (Isaiah 6:5). Before that, he was saying, "Woe are *you*. You are undone." Something happened to his nature that caused him to cry out because of his woe. Isaiah's firsthand revelation changed his life.

### How Do You Get a Firsthand Revelation?

First of all, you have to admit that you don't have a firsthand revelation before you can get it.

All my life, my dad taught me things. He taught me how to witness. He taught me how to put on the Singing Christmas Tree programs for which my church has become well-known. He taught me how to give an altar call. He didn't specifically "teach" me, but I learned those things by watching him.

Then one day, the God of my father, H. W. Barnett, became the God of *my* time and life, and what I saw and caught became a firsthand revelation.

Why should you be content with someone else's experience? There has to be a time when you aren't content, even though you are doing signs and miracles. There has to come a time when you want to have a revelation for yourself.

Some people don't come to this point easily. They are like Peter; they have to fail before they can really see Jesus.

Notice it was Peter who said, **Thou art the Christ, the Son of the living God** (Matthew 16:16), and the same man to whom Jesus said, **...flesh and blood hath not revealed it unto thee...** (v. 17). Peter had even walked on water — at least for a short way. (Matthew 14:29.)

Yet Peter still denied Christ and cursed. (Mark 14:66-72.) It took Peter's failure to bring him to a firsthand revelation of himself and of Jesus. He began to weep bitterly, and his weeping brought a revelation of himself. Failure broke him, and through the broken barriers, he came to a knowledge of Christ that he hadn't received before.

Many in the Church are like a bunch of parrots running around copying what successful leaders are doing. Some of them are able to pull it off, based on what has been imparted to them. But I believe many children of God are beginning to wake up and seek a firsthand revelation. I want them to have what God has for them, and you to have everything God has for you.

My children used to think I was the smartest man in the world. But the older they got, apparently the dumber I had gotten!

There was a time when they said, "Dad, what is this? What is that?" I would tell them out of my knowledge. Then a time came when they said, "Dad, I know."

I would say, "Son, you do it this way."

"I know, Dad!"

"Son, before you start the car, you put it...."

"I know, Daddy."

I felt sometimes like saying, "If you say 'I know' one more time!..." (all in Christian love, of course).

They had simply received firsthand revelations about life, instead of secondhand knowledge imparted by me. That's a part of growing up, and it's also a part of growing up in the Lord.

In Matthew 11:25 NAS Jesus said:

**I praise Thee, O Father, Lord of heaven and earth, that Thou didst hide these things from the wise and intelligent and didst reveal them to babes.**

The problem with Bible schools, colleges and seminaries is that people come out with theological terminology. It used to be *salvation*; now it's *theology*. It used to be the *coming of the Lord Jesus Christ*; now it's the *eschatological understanding of the last days*.

The fact is: if people don't know personally what they are talking about, they tend to talk theologically or theoretically. If the revelations are a part of them, they tend to express that knowledge in simpler language, their own words. (I'm not against big words; I'm talking about a principle of revelation.)

Jesus didn't use the terminology of the religious leaders of His day. He talked about thieves, goats, wheat, sores, bread, leaven and salt. He said, except you come as a little child, you can't enter the kingdom. (Mark 10:15.) Babies are filled with wonder.

In order to get a firsthand revelation, you must become as a little child. You must say: "God, I can't live with a secondhand revelation. I can't take the chance that because I was raised in church, because my mama taught me the Bible, because I prayed and heard sermons, I really *know* You."

If you will draw nigh to Him and turn your life over to Him, He will give you a firsthand revelation. *Then* you can begin to become an impacting man and really take the kingdom by force!

# 4

# A LOVE FOR GOD, HIS PEOPLE, AND HIS WORD

*If you have a divine call to the ministry, you must prove it. Does everyone who is spiritual recognize that call?*

**–Karl Strader**

4

## *A LOVE FOR GOD, HIS PEOPLE, AND HIS WORD*

### by Karl Strader
*Pastor, Carpenter's Home Church*
*Lakeland, Florida*

There's a problem facing the church today that I call "spiritual AIDS," and I want to share what I feel is the antidote: We need an all-encompassing love for God, a love for His Word, and a love for His people.

The disease of "spiritual AIDS" can be detected by four prominent symptoms:

1. Accusation
2. Intimidation
3. Deception
4. Self-exaltation

A friend of mine who has pastored a church in Atlanta for twenty-eight years never had any trouble with anyone until the early part of 1988. At that time, some of the "pillars" in the church began to rise up and question his integrity. People on his board suddenly began to ask ridiculous questions that had never been asked before.

*Everyone*, not just the IRS, seems to be questioning preachers today. The people sitting in the pews are questioning. Many of them are angry. Some of them are getting hostile. To tell you the truth, given the way some preachers have acted in the past several years, I think people have a right to be angry.

My daughter Carla is my secretary and reads all my letters. One day she asked me something that I couldn't answer, mostly because I didn't want to; I was too ashamed. She said, "Daddy, look at the way some of these preachers are acting [writing and talking]. People in the world don't even do that, do they?"

God is looking for people today who will stand up for that which is decent and right. He does *not* want His Body to come down with an epidemic of "spiritual AIDS." That isn't decent *or* right.

There is a verse in 2 Timothy that applies to everyone who is some type of Christian worker. It says:

**But watch thou in all things, endure afflictions, do the work of an evangelist,** *make full proof of thy ministry.*

**2 Timothy 4:5**

### Endure Afflictions

When Paul wrote **...watch thou in all things...,** he was talking about watching out for the devil, because the enemy is involved in all matters pertaining to darkness and destruction. Those four symptoms that we have seen manifested as a "disease" in the Church in recent years are certainly not of God, but of the devil.

I no longer believe one of the principles I was taught in seminary: that there are works of the devil and works of the flesh. I'm totally convinced that there is no work of the flesh that isn't the work of the devil.

For example, one of the works of the flesh listed in Galatians 5:20 is *witchcraft.* There is no way that this work of the flesh could exist apart from the devil. Perhaps Finis Jennings Dake made some mistakes in his annotated version of the Bible; however, I believe him when he said that behind every unholy trait is demon power, and behind every sickness or disease is demon power.*

In 1 Peter 5:8, Peter also tells us to *watch out.* He's talking about being sober and vigilant because your adversary isn't flesh and blood. Our adversary, the devil, is walking about as a roaring lion seeking whom he may devour.

I used to think that whenever you got to be about sixty years of age, it would be like riding a horse and turning it toward the barn. It would just be an easy ride on into home. But as I have discovered, that just isn't so. The ride simply gets harder the farther you go. Your problems just multiply through the years.

Truer words were never spoken than Paul's in 2 Timothy 4:5: **...endure afflictions....** Then in Psalm 34:19, it says:

**Many are the afflictions of the righteous: but the Lord delivereth him out of them all.**

If you have a divine call to the ministry, you must prove it. Does everyone who is spiritual recognize that call? Does God recognize that call, or did your parents or perhaps your spouse call you?

God help us to find out if we truly have a call from Him and then, if we do, to make full proof of our ministries!

If you are called as an evangelist, the proof will be the fruit of souls that remains after you leave town.

If you are called to pastor, it takes ten to fifteen years to build a church. It takes that long for the townspeople to see how you treat your wife and whether or not you exhibit personal integrity. Most communities also want to see what kind of a parent you are with your children. After you have proven yourself and have won your right

---

*Finis Jennings Dake. *Annotated Reference Bible.* (Lawrenceville, GA: Dake's Bible Sales, 1963).

to be heard, then people will start coming to church. But they want to watch you for a while.

If you're going to make full proof of your ministry as a pastor, you can't pastor a church for a couple of years and then move on to build another church. You have to "hang in there."

## You Must Love God

In order to fulfill any divine call rightly, the first thing you must do is love God. If you love Him, you will prove it by doing everything He says.

Every time you come across a commandment, *do it.* It doesn't mean a thing if you say you love God, but you don't keep His commandments. Jesus said in John 14:21:

**He that hath my commandments, and keepeth them, he it is that loveth me: and he that loveth me shall be loved of my Father, and I will love him, and will manifest myself to him.**

## Be Sold Out for God

I first came to God when I was eight years old at a rural Methodist church in Homestead, a small town in western Oklahoma. (I grew up in the "Dust Bowl" era, so I know what life was like during that time.)

That year, an old-fashioned evangelist came to our church from Asbury College in Kentucky and preached in that little church. I got saved during one of his meetings.

There were probably thirty people in my whole town, not counting the cows that roamed the streets. Talk about a nobody from nowhere — that was me! So that was my early life — brought up in the wheat fields during the Depression.

My mother must have had some Baptist in her, because she made that preacher baptize me by immersion in a nearby muddy creek. I can still see him testing the creek bottom with a crooked stick while I stood on the bank with tears streaming down my cheeks. I knew what I was doing and what baptism meant: I was telling the world that I had given my heart to Jesus.

Then during the summer that I was sixteen, I went to a Methodist youth camp at Turner Falls, Oklahoma. One night the youth were dancing. Since my little church didn't believe in that, I wandered away by myself from the rest of the campers and began to pray. That night, as a sophomore in high school, I sold out to Jesus lock, stock and barrel.

From that moment until now, I don't remember having any kind of ambition of my own. I can't remember having a dream or vision of my own. My whole soul, body, spirit, and life have been wrapped up in the Lord Jesus Christ. I sold out *everything* to God.

I love God, and I don't want to hurt Him. I don't want to displease Him, especially at this time of my life. All through my life, I haven't cared much for the applause of men. I really care about only one thing: to win God's smile of approval — because I love Him.

If you are going to say, as Thomas did, **...My Lord and my God** (John 20:28), you ought to mean those words from the bottom of your heart. And you really need that kind of revelation if you are going to minister to others. Prostrate yourself before the Lord. Sell out every inch of your body, your soul, and your spirit to the love of God.

The *first and great commandment*, according to Jesus, is found in Matthew 22:37,38:

**...Thou shalt love the Lord thy God with all thy heart, and with all thy soul, and with all thy mind.**

**This is the first and great commandment.**

It will save you so much stress and heartache, and it will mean so much in the midst of storms *for the rest of your life* if you are sold out to the lordship of Jesus. When you are completely sold out to Jesus, you will realize that you have also sold out to the Father and the Holy Spirit — one God manifested in three Persons. His name is Wonderful, Counselor, the mighty God, the everlasting Father and the Prince of Peace. (Isaiah 9:6.)

### You Must Love People

If you have an all-encompassing love for Jesus, that will first of all mean that you have a sweet spirit toward other people as well.

**Charity suffereth long, and is kind; charity envieth not; charity vaunteth not itself, is not puffed up,**

**Doth not behave itself unseemly, seeketh not her own, is not easily provoked, thinketh no evil;**

**Rejoiceth not in iniquity, but rejoiceth in the truth;**

**Beareth all things, believeth all things, hopeth all things, endureth all things.**

**1 Corinthians 13:4-7**

These verses describe what it means to have a sweet spirit. If you and I as ministers ever get hostile with our people, that isn't God; that's the devil.

If we start accusing people, that isn't God either; that's the devil. It's called *railing* in the Bible (1 Peter 3:9). God wants all railing to stop!

God wants us to stop manifesting that first symptom of "spiritual AIDS" — accusation. If we can't give a word of encouragement to someone, let's just keep our mouths shut.

However, exhibiting a sweet spirit to others isn't all there is to loving God.

Second, we ought to walk in the kind of love that stops and helps a man lying by the side of the road instead of running on to our committee meeting.

**But whoso hath this world's good, and seeth his brother have need, and shutteth up his bowels of compassion from him, how dwelleth the love of God in him?**

1 John 3:17

According to this verse, one aspect of loving God is to visit prisons. An old college friend of mine wrote in his doctoral thesis that no great man of God ever lived who hadn't preached on the street or in jail.

If you never preach on the street or in jail, you will never be a great man of God — that is, if the track record of the past is any indication. All of the great spiritual leaders in history preached in those two places.

Jesus said that if we truly have the love of God in our hearts, we will visit those in prison and those who are sick; we will clothe the naked, feed the hungry, and get them something to drink in the name of Jesus. (Matthew 25:34-36.) We must do something to relieve the hurts of mankind if we really have the love of God in our hearts. It isn't enough just to say, "I love you — 'bye!"

The third aspect of manifesting the love of God toward other people is to be tolerant. We need to recognize that we are only a *part* of the Body of Christ. The Lord has more than just a Word church, or a faith church, or a confession church, or a denominational church, or an independent church. God has other people out there who belong to the Body of Christ, and we have to love them.

In fact, we must love *all* Christians — and that takes the love of God! No one can do that on his own. We need to be tolerant even of the cults, for how will we ever have the opportunity to win them if we only show hostility toward them? Even people of other religions shouldn't be castigated.

## Love Means Tolerance

If we love God, we will be tolerant of everyone else in His world. Tolerance helps us to be the kind of Christian others will respect. They can look at us and perhaps come to believe in what we stand for. But if we ridicule other denominations, religions, cults, or even the occult world, how will people ever be persuaded to listen to us?

Our job is to win people to Jesus, to turn them on to righteousness. But the average man on the street today has a better idea of what a *real* Christian ought to be than some of us who are believers! Almost any bartender can tell a real Christian when he sees one, but some of us wonder who is a Christian and who isn't.

Ask the man on the street. Ask the IRS. They can tell you who is and who isn't a Christian!

Being a real Christian isn't something you can gain by works. It isn't something you can be taught. It is something you must feel in your spirit and your soul by the Holy Spirit. That's the love of God.

Jesus said that if any would come after Him, they must deny themselves, take up their "cross" daily and follow Him. (Matthew 16:24.) In other words, it's a complete sellout. If you truly love Jesus, you will follow Him and no one else.

When I was called to preach, I was a senior in college and no longer a Methodist. I was attending a Pentecostal church by that time. I had always wanted to marry a Pentecostal girl, because back in those days, they always had their faces washed clean, and I wanted to see what I was getting! So I started attending a Pentecostal church, and I got my Pentecostal girl. Then God baptized me in the Holy Spirit.

At that time, I had been waiting since I was eight for a call from God to the ministry. I wanted to preach, but I knew I had to have the call.

## A Love for God, His People, and His Word

One day I was sitting in a chapel service among about three thousand other people. The speaker for the service had just returned from a trip to Europe. All of a sudden, it was as if God took His great big hand and gripped me around my heart. Really, it felt like a heart attack. I had never had one, but I had heard people describe heart attacks. It was rough! But I knew it was God.

Very quietly, I said, "God, what is it?"

He said, "Would you preach My Word?"

I answered, "God, You know that ever since I was a little kid I have wanted to preach, but I was waiting for You to let me know."

Then He said, "I'm calling you now."

I said yes, and the pressure lifted. From that day to this, I have never questioned the call to preach.

I have pastored at my church in Lakeland for more than thirty years. But if the board of deacons suggested that I resign, and if the congregation went along with the board and I had no other place to go, I don't believe that would stop me from preaching.

The love of God is in my heart, and so is the call of God. Therefore, I will preach whether I have a pulpit to stand behind or not. There are plenty of street corners in America and plenty of radio stations I could get on. I would find some way to preach the Gospel.

Many prisons today will let you come in to preach, and that means a lot of captive audiences! I believe there are more Christians in prisons today than ever before. It's amazing how many people Charles Colson has gotten saved in prisons, as well as all the other ministries that minister to those in prison. It's wonderful!

But if you are called, you *have* to preach. All the devils in hell can't stop you, because the love of God constrains you. It's the love of God that helps you love people enough to want to minister to them and get their hurts healed. It's the love of God that doesn't let you give up until their lives are turned around and they are headed the right way.

Besides loving God and loving others, you must love yourself — but not too much. The Bible says that when you come to Jesus, you are to *deny* yourself. (Luke 9:23.) So for a real Christian, there really is no such thing as self-esteem, self-worth, or even self-image. You are to be lost in Jesus and become *His* image. Self is to die. So how can you get high and mighty esteeming something that's already dead? You must balance Scripture against Scripture.

We are to love our neighbor *as ourselves*. Yet the Word says that **...in the last days...men will be lovers of self...** (2 Timothy 3:1,2 NAS), and that's bad. So we love ourselves — but not too much. We don't love ourselves enough to be selfish, but enough to have self-respect, because Jesus loved us enough to die for us. We are worth something to the Godhead.

So we are to die out to self, but maintain self-respect. We are to love ourselves enough to live right, to stand true to God and His Word, and to stay pure and holy in every area of our lives.

## Love Means Setting an Example

You and I have no ground to stand on to convince someone else to live a Christian life if we aren't living the Christian life ourselves. Our priorities must be first our relationship with God and then with our spouse.

Today there is an all-out attack on the wives of pastors and evangelists. Several years ago, I discovered that an intercessor in my church was praying for my wife to die. Two other ladies were praying that my wife would live, doing battle for her in the Spirit; therefore, they were included in the "death prayer."

## A Love for God, His People, and His Word

When I found out about the situation, I tried to cast the devil out of that false intercessor. But I couldn't get the woman to let go of that spirit of witchcraft, so I followed Dr. Cho's advice: If you can't get the devil out of a person, cast both the devil and that person out of your church! That's what I had to do.

After that incident, God got hold of my heart and said: "You haven't been doing your part. You are the high priest of your home. You should not depend on intercessors to protect your wife. You need to be doing that."

He also told me that, as senior pastor, I needed to protect the intercessors of my church from the witchcraft that has crept into the church in the guise of intercession.

As Christians, we need to watch today as never before, because Satan knows his time is very, very short. He's a defeated foe, and you and I need to keep our armor on and our swords ready. Don't ever think a roaring lion doesn't bite! He has just as many teeth as those lions that don't roar.

God wants those of us who are pastors to be protectors for our spouses and for the other people in our church. Let's take our authority and put the devil to flight!

It used to be that when I got up in the morning, I would wonder what the devil was going to do to me that day. Now he wonders what *I'm* going to do to *him*! That's the way every Christian ought to live.

One time, a counselor was casting devils out of a girl in our church, and I walked into the counseling room to see how she was doing. A voice was speaking through the girl's mouth, as demons sometimes do. Then the counselor said, "*Now*, the senior pastor is here!" and the devil screamed out in another voice, "Oh! You didn't tell me the senior pastor was coming in here."

Well, God wants the senior pastor, the undershepherd of the Lord Jesus Christ, in the middle of a situation once in a while to let the devil know who's in charge of things!

## The Body Has Many Parts

In our household, my wife comes first, and then the children. I believe that all four of my children are saved today for two reasons: I prayed with them, and I played with them. For years, Thursdays have been my "sabbaths" — my rest days. We had family worship every day, and every Thursday was reserved for family time and relaxation.

I challenge every man or woman of God to love your family enough to pray with them every day and to take a day off each week to spend quality time with them. I know it helps. Today all of my children are saved and filled with the Holy Spirit. Three of them work with me, and I have four grandchildren who are being raised in the knowledge of God.

There's no way to get around it: If we take Communion and don't discern the Body of Christ according to the love of God, we are in trouble. For example, if you or I speak evil of others and hold resentment in our hearts and then take Communion, we are in trouble.

I have seen a lot of people die before their time because they didn't discern the Body of Christ. Many Christians are guilty of the sin of not discerning the *whole* body. We need everyone.

Wouldn't it be wonderful if every Pentecostal could be handcuffed to a Baptist? The Pentecostals are always losing their salvation, and the Baptists never lose theirs, so that would give us a balance!

Pentecostals say, "Hallelujah," and Presbyterians say, "Shut up; that isn't necessary." If we put the two together, we would have a balance. Catholics reverence the ministry and believe in miracles, signs and wonders, whereas many Protestants today do neither. So, we need each other in the Body of Christ.

We must learn to discern Christ's Body because very soon He will be bringing it together in unity. I don't know *how* He is going to do that. Perhaps it will take persecution.

Because of events that have transpired in the Body of Christ over the past several years, it has seemed as if unity suffered a setback of about thirty years. But I believe the tide is running the other way now.

Someone said, "I hope I never see 1987 again," but I hope I never see the events of the past several years again! It has been rugged for the church, but I don't believe it is just because of television evangelists.

I believe that a war is being fought in the heavenlies. I think the devil knows his time is short. The world is getting worse and worse, but the church is getting better and better. If Jesus delays His coming, then the church is going to have one of the greatest revivals and harvests of souls it has seen in all of church history.

I believe this with all my heart. But if we're going to get the Gospel to the ends of the earth, we must love God, His body, and all men.

There are no "ifs, ands, or buts" about it; if you and I aren't missionary-minded, we have missed God. We will never amount to a hill of beans if we don't give to missions.

So we must love God and love people. First, we must love the household of faith. Then we must love the unsaved. Third, we must love the written Word.

## You Must Love the Word

What do you think about when you say or hear "the Word"? Do you think *the Bible*? You need to think *Jesus*; He is the living Word.

The apostle John said that Jesus is the Word:

**In the beginning was the Word, and the Word was with God, and the Word was God.**

**John 1:1**

The Bible says the Word is **...quick, and powerful, and sharper than any twoedged sword...** (Hebrews 4:12). Personally, I believe this verse refers to Jesus as well.

Second Timothy 3:16,17 says that not only does Scripture contain the Word of God, it *is* the Word of God. Why? Because it tells about Jesus from Genesis to Revelation. You and I won't be anchored unless we know the Word, and we won't be able to make it unless we are anchored.

**All scripture is given by inspiration of God, and is profitable for doctrine, for reproof, for correction, for instruction in righteousness:**

**That the man of God may be perfect, throughly furnished unto all good works.**

**2 Timothy 3:16,17**

From Genesis to Revelation, in whatever translation you have, the Word of God is truth. The Bible is scientifically accurate, although it isn't a scientific book. It's historically correct, although it isn't just a book of history. The Bible is God's book. It's His voice, and we can bank on the fact that it is entirely true.

We ought to memorize the Word, study the Word, and meditate upon the Word day and night.

You may say, "That's abnormal!" But it isn't. Meditating on God's written Word day and night should be a normal Christian experience for laymen — not to mention preachers!

In connection with that, let me say that we need to meditate on the Bible until it's a *living* Word on the inside of us. Otherwise, all we will have is the letter of the Law, which kills.

It's the Spirit that gives life, and we need a good hold on the living Word. *Rhema*, not just *logos*, is what we need. We need the Holy Spirit to flow through the pages.

In fact, you shouldn't try to study the Word unless you're filled with the Holy Spirit. Otherwise, you may come up with some crazy, weird dream of the devil.

God help us to depend on the Holy Spirit to help teach us about the written Word and the living Word!

To preach the Word means *to preach or to lift up Jesus* — not just to lift up the Bible, but to lift up *Jesus*. And there is no contradiction in that.

The Bible is the Word of God because it is all about Jesus. It's an anchor for each Christian. If we get away from this Word, we are likely to get away from Jesus, and then we will be finished. We ought to read "the fine print." Jesus said:

**...It is written, That man shall not live by bread alone, but by every word of God.**

**Luke 4:4**

The Bible says that whatsoever we ask in prayer *believing*, we shall receive. (Mark 11:23.) The Bible also says that we receive of Him because we keep His commandments and do what is pleasing in His sight. (1 John 3:22.) Now if we take one of these Scriptures and not the other, we haven't "read the fine print," and we are in trouble. And those of us who are pastors won't be able to lead our people rightly.

As Christians, we need *every* bit of the Word. We need to read the fine print of the contract. Then when we pray for the sick and nothing happens, as it did for Jesus in His hometown of Nazareth, we will have an answer. We will know why everyone doesn't get healed. Or if someone looks as if he is the finest Christian in the Church, but he dies a premature death, we will know why.

We must go to the Word of God through the Holy Spirit. If everyone else around us falls, the Bible still says that he who dwells in the secret place of the Most High will abide under the shadow of the Almighty. (Psalm 91:1.)

## War a Good Warfare

If I ever had pride in anything, it was in my ability to choose my friends carefully. But after all that has transpired since the late '80s, that pride is all gone.

However, in the midst of all of the turbulence and the "hullabaloo," I want everyone to know one thing: God wants us to get out of this muck we have been wading around in and have the peace that passes all understanding. (Philippians 4:7.) He wants us to have **...joy unspeakable and full of glory** (1 Peter 1:8). We ought to forget the things that are behind and press on toward the mark for the prize of the high calling in Christ Jesus. (Philippians 3:14.) *The best is yet to come!*

I see nothing but a bright future in store for the Church of the living God. If this younger generation of His children will latch onto His righteousness and keep His peace and joy in their hearts, the sky is the limit! They will so far outdo those of my generation that they will leave those of us who have been on the road for years in the dust.

God is God! Jesus, the Son of God, is available to every one of us. The Holy Spirit is here to empower us in the days ahead as we have never seen in the history of the Church. Our finest hour is just ahead.

We need to remember, however, that it is guerilla warfare all the way to the end. Our fight is not against flesh and blood, but against principalities and powers in the heavenlies. (Ephesians 6:12.)

## A Love for God, His People, and His Word

As pastors often discover, firing a troublemaker or asking the person to resign doesn't eliminate all the problems in the Church. The devil is still there, trying to stir up new problems.

Most of us pastors have had to first put out fires here and there and then build the right kind of fire in the pulpit. We have had to learn to keep the pulpit platform hot with the fire and power of God.

*(stage)*

We must war a good warfare. At all times we must have on the helmet of salvation and the breastplate of righteousness; keep our loins girded with truth and our feet shod with the preparation of the Gospel of peace; *and* hold fast to our shield of faith. (Ephesians 6:13-17.) We must have our spiritual armor in place all around us, not just in front of us as we learned in Sunday school.

Forget that particular Sunday school teaching; just watch how NASA designs space capsules to bring them safely back to earth. A heat shield completely covers the bottom of the space capsule as it returns from outer space. This shield must be able to bear the intense heat caused by the friction that results from coming through earth's atmosphere at extremely high velocities.

In a similar way, you and I need the shield of faith completely surrounding us because the devil fights dirty; he always has. He will come from any direction he can to gain access to our lives.

God wants our hearts to beat for souls as His does. If we should ever wonder why we're in the ministry or what God has called us to do, we can always know that that's the bottom line: We are called to turn people to righteousness.

In order to fulfill that divine purpose, it is our responsibility to love God, love His Word, and love people.

# 5

## *THE KEYS TO TOTAL VICTORY*

*Jesus didn't die on the Cross to give us the ability to cope, but the ability to conquer. Limited victory is not victory. God wants His people to have total victory over the enemy. And what Jesus did on the Cross has enabled us to have that total victory in every area of our lives.*

*God through Jesus has given us all we could ever need to win the battles of life and to overcome the enemy on every front. Regardless of where you are in your life today, or what battles you are facing, you can be encouraged to know that God has equipped you for total victory.*

*As you read through this chapter I pray for your faith to be energized as you realize the awesome authority God has invested in His people and the potential we have to succeed and overcome through Christ.*

**— Jimmy Evans**

## THE KEYS TO TOTAL VICTORY

by Jimmy Evans
*Pastor, Trinity Fellowship Church*
*Amarillo, Texas*

One of the realities becoming clearer every day is the level of warfare that we Christians are involved in. It's harder than ever to deny the existence and activity of Satan as he comes to resist the purposes of God in this world and in our lives. His attacks are vicious and constant. For us to live in peace and in God's will, we must learn to conquer the enemy as he would come to hinder God's will from being done in our lives.

A story in 2 Kings 13 has a powerful application to our lives and will help us to understand the keys to victory over the devil. This story is about a king of Israel who needed help to overcome his enemies. He was sincere and had every opportunity to succeed, but he didn't. His failure to act upon God's specific instruction and to seize his opportunity for total victory led to his own personal defeat, as well as the tragic downfall of the nation of Israel.

The story takes place long ago, but the mistake of the king is still a common one for believers today. When the king's mistake is repeated in our lives it causes unnecessary defeat for us and allows victory for the devil. We will see that the king was enabled by God to win a battle over his enemies, but failed to succeed. The significance of this biblical account for our day is obvious, because we are engaged in a severe spiritual battle. And even though we have been equipped by God to win, we must still make personal decisions and changes that will decide the victory.

I believe, as many do, that we are living in the end times and that believers are locked in a vicious spiritual battle. This is a high-stakes eternal struggle with Satan and his forces — for our lives, for our families, for the lost, for our cities, and for the purposes of God. We must win the fight and be victorious over the devil.

So to help us understand more clearly how to accomplish this, let's look at this important text of Scripture surrounding this disobedient Hebrew king's life that is loaded with kingdom principles and biblical patterns for total spiritual victory in 2 Kings 13:

**Elisha had become sick with the illness of which he would die. Then Joash the king of Israel came down to him, and wept over his face, and said, "O my father, my father, the chariots of Israel and their horsemen!"**

**And Elisha said to him, "Take a bow and some arrows." So he took himself a bow and some arrows.**

**Then he said to the king of Israel, "Put your hand on the bow." So he put his hand on it, and Elisha put his hands on the king's hands.**

**And he said, "Open the east window"; and he opened it. Then Elisha said, "Shoot"; and he shot. And he said, "The arrow of the LORD's deliverance and the arrow of deliverance from Syria; for you must strike the Syrians at Aphek till you have destroyed them."**

**Then he said, "Take the arrows"; so he took them. And he said to the king of Israel, "Strike the ground"; so he struck three times, and stopped.**

**And the man of God was angry with him, and said, "You should have struck five or six times; then you**

would have struck Syria till you had destroyed it! But now you will strike Syria only three times."

Then Elisha died, and they buried him. And the raiding bands from Moab invaded the land in the spring of the year.

So it was, as they were burying a man, that suddenly they spied a band of raiders; and they put the man in the tomb of Elisha; and when the man was let down and touched the bones of Elisha, he revived and stood on his feet.

2 Kings 13:14-21 NKJV

## King Joash Visits Elisha

This is a very powerful story.

First of all, King Joash comes to visit Elisha the prophet. In the Old Testament, it was extremely unusual for a king to visit a prophet. Typically, a prophet met with a king to give him a word from God; and many times the only reason a king visited a prophet was to persecute or kill him. But in this case, Elisha is about to die, so the king pays him a visit to receive a word from the Lord.

When the king arrives at Elisha's bedside, he says some interesting words to Elisha in verse 14 NKJV: **...O my father, my father, the chariots of Israel and their horsemen!** Now these may seem like strange words to say to a sick man who is about to die. But they are the same words Elisha spoke when he saw the prophet Elijah departing the earth in a chariot of fire. Elisha shouted, **...My father, my father, the chariot of Israel and its horsemen!** (2 Kings 2:12 NKJV.)

It's probable that King Joash knows that Elisha had said this; Elisha was a popular figure, and so was Elijah. But I believe there are two other possibilities as to why Joash says these words to Elisha.

First, Joash is trying to appeal to Elisha's sense of mercy. You see, Joash knows that Elisha felt insecure when he saw Elijah leaving in the chariot of fire. Elisha had known that God's power and protection were with Elijah, following him wherever he went. So when Elisha saw Elijah leaving, you can imagine how insecure he must have felt.

Second, Joash says those words because he knows Elisha is constantly attended by chariots of fire from God. Joash is afraid that when Elisha dies, God's protection will be removed from Israel and they will be conquered by their enemies, the Syrians.

In 2 Kings 6, we see why Joash knows that chariots of fire are with Elisha. Here is the story of the Syrian king who finds out that Elisha is telling secrets about him to the king of Israel. The king of Syria says to the men around him, "Which of you is a traitor, who shares my secrets with the king of Israel?" They answer, "It isn't us, king. Israel has a secret weapon: the prophet Elisha. He's telling the king of Israel what you are saying in your bedroom." (Author's paraphrase, vv. 11,12.)

So the Syrian king sends men by night to surround the house of Elisha. When Elisha's servant wakes up the next morning, he sees the army surrounding the house. He says to Elisha, "The army of Syria is surrounding our house! What shall we do?" (Author's paraphrase, v. 15.) But Elisha isn't disturbed. There isn't one bit of panic in his voice as he replies: "Lord, I pray that the eyes of my servant be opened to see that those who are with us are more than those who are with the Syrians." (Author's paraphrase, v. 17.)

You see, if our eyes are opened, we will understand that the army of God is greater than the army of the enemy. If only a third of the angels of heaven fell, that means we have two times more holy angels on our side than the devil has fallen angels on his side! Besides, the power of God is infinitely greater than the power of the enemy!

When Elisha prays for his servant, the servant's eyes are suddenly opened, and he sees that the mountains of Israel are covered with chariots of fire! Elisha is attended by God's army!

So now when King Joash comes to Elisha, I believe that he is trying to identify with the dying prophet. He knows Elisha is about to die. He understands how important Elisha has been to Israel's national security and that God's blessing and protection have been with Israel because of Elisha.

Joash is fearful of what the menacing Syrian army will do when they hear that the secret weapon of Israel is gone. So he cries out, **...O my father, my father, the chariots of Israel and their horsemen!** He is saying to Elisha: "Don't take God's heavenly hosts with you when you die. Don't leave this nation unprotected. You know what it's like to have someone depart, to be insecure and fearful that you will be left alone and unprotected. I'm saying to you what you said to your predecessor."

This strikes a chord with Elisha. It's something he can identify with. So he gets up off his deathbed and enables King Joash to conquer the Syrians. Not only is Elisha fulfilling Joash's request for his blessing of protection, he is also going one step further. Elisha is enabling Joash and the Israelites to become conquerors and to live in perpetual, generational victory.

## A Type of Christ

There is something you need to understand about Elisha. In the account we've just discussed and in his ministry, Elisha is a type of Jesus Christ.

When you look in the Old Testament at the patriarchs and the giants of the faith, you will see strength and anointing in their lives. This quality in a biblical character is always a type of Christ. If you took all the characters of the Bible and wrapped them together, you would see a composite of Christ. So Elisha is a foreshadowing of the ministry of Jesus Christ.

First, like Jesus, Elisha had compassion on the sinner. For example, King Joash wasn't a godly man, and he came from an ungodly line. He wasn't a righteous king, and neither were his father or grandfather.

But Joash says to Elisha, "We don't deserve your blessing, but, please, my father, have mercy on my soul; bless me." So Elisha, as a type of Christ, has compassion on Joash.

Look at what Hebrews 4:15,16 NKJV says about the ministry of Jesus:

**For we do not have a High Priest who cannot sympathize with our weaknesses, but was in all points tempted as we are, yet without sin.**

**Let us therefore come boldly to the throne of grace, that we may obtain mercy and find grace to help in time of need.**

Jesus is a merciful Savior. Whenever we have a need in our lives, He welcomes us to come to Him, and He identifies with us, as Elisha identifies with King Joash in this account. So this is an important issue.

Second, Elisha in his death equips the king for victory, just as Jesus did for us through His death. Colossians 2:13-15 NKJV tells us how Jesus' death has enabled us for victory:

**And you, being dead in your trespasses and the uncircumcision of your flesh, He has made alive together with Him, having forgiven you all trespasses, having wiped out the handwriting of requirements that was against us, which was contrary to us. And He has taken it out of the way, having nailed it to the cross.**

116

**Having disarmed principalities and powers, He made a public spectacle of them, triumphing over them in it.**

These verses say that Jesus Christ has taken all of our sins and nailed them to the Cross, disarming the condemnation and the power that Satan has over us through our sins. It also says that through the Cross, Jesus disarmed principalities, stripped them of their armor and their weapons, and made a public spectacle of them. In His death, Jesus enabled us to achieve total victory.

We see Elisha doing the same thing for Joash. Elisha gets up off his deathbed and enables the king to win.

Third, there is a resurrection after Elisha's death. Second Kings 13:20,21 tells us a most unusual story. When Elisha dies, his spirit goes to paradise, but his body is laid in a grave. Then a band of raiders comes by. Some people have a body to bury, but when they see the raiders, rather than taking the time to dig a grave, they drop the body into Elisha's grave. And the dead man is resurrected when he touches Elisha's bones!

This account is further evidence that Elisha was a man anointed of God. The resurrection after Elisha's death attests to his office, to his anointing, and to the fact that Elisha was a type of Christ.

## Elisha Equips the King for Victory

King Joash says, **...O my father, my father, the chariots of Israel and their horsemen!** (v. 14 NKJV). Elisha answers, "Take a bow and some arrows," so Joash puts an arrow in the bow.

Then Elisha puts his arms around the king and places his hands on the king's hands, saying, "Now open the window." So the king opens the window, and when that arrow leaves the bow, it's under the combined power of the man of God and the king. As it flies out the window,

117

Elisha says, "The arrow of the Lord's deliverance, for you must go and strike the Syrians until you totally defeat them." (Author's paraphrase, vv. 15-17.)

## An Anointed Word

Elisha gets up off his deathbed and gives Joash an anointed word. He says in essence, "I'm telling you what God's will is for this battle. I'm giving you a word of direction on how you can conquer the enemy. You must strike the Syrians until they are utterly destroyed."

In the same way, Jesus is the Anointed Word of God. For every circumstance in our lives in which we need victory, God wants to give us an anointed word.

That's why the Bible is so thick. God has an anointed word for victory in *every* area of your life — in your physical body, your thinking, your marriage, your family, your finances, your ministry, your past, your present, and your future.

## An Anointed Weapon

Elisha gives Joash an anointed weapon: the arrow of the Lord's deliverance. He says, "This arrow (which is symbolic of the army of Israel) is the Lord's deliverance."

Whenever we are locked in a battle with the devil, it is vitally important to understand that God has a weapon for us to use in every battle. Our primary weapon is the Word of God. According to Ephesians 6, the Word is the sword of the Spirit, and it's *always* ready for battle. Other powerful weapons include the Name of Jesus, the Blood of Jesus, and prayer.

Now we don't always use the same weapon. God has an anointed weapon for *every* battle. Sometimes His weapon for our battle is prayer. Other times there is a person anointed to minister and stand with us in the particular area of our need, so God sends that person to us with the anointing. Sometimes His weapon is the confession that we make. At other times, God reveals His will to us and our obedience to His Word overcomes the enemy.

I remember when I wanted to stop smoking more than twenty years ago. I tried a hundred times to stop, using every method I knew, but I couldn't. Then the Holy Spirit spoke to my heart, "Say you're a nonsmoker." Making that confession is how I stopped. God's weapon for my battle was an anointed confession.

## An Anointed Warrior

Elisha reveals to Joash that the weapon is the army of Israel. He is saying: "The weapon is your aggression against the enemy. Now *you* be an anointed warrior; *you* go and strike the enemy."

In Matthew 16:19, Jesus says: "I have given *you* the keys to the kingdom of heaven. Whatever you bind on earth will be bound in heaven; whatever you loose on earth will be loosed in heaven."

Ephesians 6:11 tells us to take up the full armor of God. Why? Because we are in a battle. We are warriors in the army of Almighty God. We need an anointed word. We need an anointed weapon. We need to become an anointed warrior.

Elisha totally enables the king for victory. It's interesting to see what happens at this point.

## The King Fails To Be Victorious

In 2 Kings 13:18,19 Elisha says to the king, "Take the arrows and strike the ground," so the king strikes the ground three times, then looks at Elisha. But Elisha is angry. He says: "If you had struck the ground five or six times, you would have utterly destroyed the enemy. But because you have struck the ground only three times, you will have only three victories over your enemy. (Author's paraphrase.) As history records, that's what happened. The Israelites had only three victories over their archenemies the Syrians before the tables turned against them.

At this point, I have two comments to make.

First, Jesus didn't die on the Cross to give us the ability to cope, but the ability to conquer. Limited victory is not victory. God wants His people to have *total* victory over the enemy. And what Jesus did on the Cross has enabled us to enjoy that total victory in every area of our lives.

Second, God through Jesus has given us all we could ever need to win the battles of life and to overcome the enemy. He has given us *anointed words*, not only through the Bible but also through the *rhema* word He speaks in our heart. He has given us *anointed weapons*, such as His Word, His Name, and the gifts of the Holy Spirit. And He has made us to be *anointed warriors* for Him.

In Matthew 28:18,19 Jesus is saying: "All authority has been given to Me in heaven and on earth, and I give you My authority. You have the authority of Almighty God to go all over the earth and to preach this Gospel. Go, therefore." So Jesus has totally equipped every believer for victory.

Now let me tell you what we have to do.

Elisha did everything he could for the king to become totally equipped for victory. Yet Joash was not victorious. He was half-hearted, lukewarm, compromising. When he only apathetically struck the ground, the results were a rebuke from Elisha and a lack of victory.

I believe this is also true about many of the Lord's people today. They love the Lord. They believe in His power and His promises. They know what the Word says about the Cross and about their victory over Satan.

But they have not united what they know and believe with a zealous, overcoming faith.

First John 5:4 NKJV tells us, **...And this is the victory that has overcome the world — our faith.** Hebrews 11:6 says that without faith it's impossible to please God. We must have faith in what God's Word says.

I'm saying to you that with any battle you have to face now or in the future, God has an anointed Word, He has an anointed weapon, and He will anoint you as a warrior for total victory. There will never be a hopeless situation or one that is outside the scope of what Jesus did on the Cross in order to give you the ability to overcome.

Jesus says, **...lo, I am with you always, even to the end of the age** (Matthew 28:20 NKJV). In other words, He is telling us, "You will never be without My anointing, My presence, or My power." He also says, **Behold, I give you the authority to trample on serpents and scorpions, and over all the power of the enemy....** (Luke 10:19 NKJV).

When talking to the Church, Jesus is so optimistic, so positive. He tells us, "You can have the power. Bind it, and it will be bound. Loose it, and it will be loosed." (Author's paraphrase, Matthew 18:18.)

So as Christians in God's army, we live in a critical time. We need to understand that we have been equipped for *total* victory, but we must put faith in what God has done for us in every battle that we face, lest we become like King Joash.

### Four Keys for Total Victory

Using this story of Elisha and King Joash, I will share four keys for total victory. Applying these keys to your life is what it takes to fully utilize the resources and opportunities for the victory God has made available to you.

**1. Total victory comes when our spirit is in harmony with God's Spirit.**

God saw the Syrians as a sinful people. Their nation was full of abominations. They were persecutors of God's people. God didn't merely dislike what was going on with them, nor was He just a little concerned about them. He was angry, and His wrath had come to full fruition; He was ready for judgment to fall upon those enemies so they would be totally destroyed.

God through His prophet Elisha tells King Joash how to bring judgment upon the Syrians, but Joash taps the ground apathetically. I don't think he hated the Syrians quite enough to win the battle. That's when he hears this rebuke from Elisha: "If you had struck the ground five or six times, you would have had total victory; but because you stopped after only three times, there will be only partial victory."

Let me ask you some questions for which I believe you will know the answers. First, how does God feel in his heart about Satan today?

Maybe He is in heaven, looking down on Satan, and He says: "You know, I really feel sorry for the devil. I know I got angry when he misbehaved in My presence in eternity past; I lost My temper and kicked him out of heaven. But he's in bad shape now. He's had a really sad life. I think it's time we started the healing process."

Is that how God feels about the devil today? No! First John 3:8 says that Jesus came to destroy the works of the devil. In God's eyes, there is nothing cute about the devil. Satan gets no sympathy from God. There is no repentance for the devil. God wants only one thing for Satan: destruction.

When we look at the problems in our lives, at lost people around us, and at all the destruction the devil has caused in this world, if we feel anything less than hatred for the devil, we will never win! Our spirit must get in tune with God's Spirit.

The truth is, many Christians sympathize with sin. They don't really believe the devil is as evil as he is. But I'm telling you, he is a destroyer of lives. He hates everything God loves; and anything that is holy to God, he hates all the more.

What Jesus said is true: The devil comes *only* to kill, to steal and to destroy. (John 10:10.) He *never* comes to bless or to help, and he will jump on us at our weakest moment. So God hates the devil!

Let me ask another question: How much does God want us to live in victory? He wanted it enough to sacrifice the life of His Son, Jesus.

God doesn't want us "hanging by our fingernails" in life. He doesn't want us coping or compromising. He doesn't want us to be praying for the Rapture just so we can get out of this life of misery. He wants us to conquer and to live in victory!

The Bible says, "If the Son sets you free, you shall be free indeed." (John 8:36.) But even though Jesus died to set you free from sin, you won't be free unless you want to be. How bad do you want it? If you don't really want to be free as a man of God or a woman of God, you'll just play at it.

But that isn't what Jesus says to do. In Matthew 11:12, NIV, He says, **From the days of John the Baptist until now, the kingdom of heaven has been forcefully advancing, and forceful men lay hold of it.** In the *King James Version*, it says, **...and the violent take it by force.**

The kingdom of God isn't for people who can't make up their minds about what they want. It's for people who have sworn off the world and have given total allegiance to God. True believers know that they will never go back; there will be no compromise.

I have made the decision to live for God; I'm not going to coexist with the devil. I refuse to allow the enemy to live in my body, in my mind, in my marriage, or in my city. I will overcome Satan in the name of Jesus Christ. The violent take it by force!

Years ago, a man asked me, "Jimmy, why is your church growing so much? What's your secret?" This man believed basically that God saves whomever He will and that there really isn't much we can do about it.

According to this man's belief, if God calls you, you will come into the kingdom, but if He doesn't, you won't. If what he believed was true, there would be no reason to evangelize. We would simply stand back and see who comes in.

This man had had a congregation of about fifty people for many years, but he had watched our church grow to more than four thousand people in a relatively short period of time. So he wanted to know the secret to our growth.

I told him, "We want our city worse than the devil wants it, so we're out beating the bushes. We're aggressive. We preach the Gospel to every creature."

Lest I and my church take credit ourselves for our rapid growth, I must say it isn't because of us that we have grown; it's because of God's grace that we are forcefully taking our city.

I'm not letting the devil have a vote by asking his opinion. It has already been decided: Jesus has all authority in Amarillo, Texas. The violent take it by force. It's the aggressive ones who are rewarded in the kingdom of God.

Talking to His Church in Revelation 3:14-22, Jesus exalts the character trait of zeal. He is speaking to the church at Laodicea, which is the last of the seven churches He addresses. Many scholars believe the church of Laodicea represents the church of this age, of these last days. Jesus doesn't congratulate them; He rebukes them. He says:

"You think you're rich, but you're poor. You think you can see, but you're blind. You think you're well off, but you're miserable. You really think you have it made. You live in a prosperous society and have convinced yourself that everything is okay. But I'm looking beyond the outside to the inside of your soul, and I'm telling you that you aren't okay."

Then Jesus gives them the eternal prognosis of what is really wrong. He says:

"I wish you were either hot or cold, either for Me or against Me. Either make up your mind to totally get into My kingdom — to walk with Me, to serve Me, and to be hot and passionate in your zeal for me, which is My will for you — or renounce Me and live for the devil. But because you are lukewarm — neutral, compromising, apathetic — I will vomit you from My mouth."

These are severe words to the Church when Jesus says, "Your lukewarmness is so distasteful to Me that I will vomit you from My mouth." That's what Jesus thinks about apathy; it's repulsive to Him!

God didn't send His only begotten Son to die on the cross so that we could play games with Him. He didn't turn His back on His Son so that we could have a powerless religion called Christianity, with one foot in the kingdom and the other foot out of it, straddling the fence, trying to live in the best of both worlds. That's being lukewarm.

The way to get lukewarm water from a faucet is to turn on hot and cold at the same time. That's what we are doing when we can't make up our minds about who will be lord of our lives, Jesus or the devil. Will we do it the world's way, or God's way? Will we listen to what God's Word says, or what the six o'clock news says? We just can't make up our minds.

When we are lukewarm, our behavior is contaminated with ungodly, compromised thinking and living. We take out of the Bible what is convenient and live by that; then we take what we want from the world and live by that. Jesus says, "That's lukewarm, and it won't get you where you want to go. I want you to be zealous, passionate, and hot."

For us to achieve our destiny and to receive the promise God has given us, we have to be sold out to Him. We have to say no to the world and die to our flesh, saying, "I am crucified to the world. I stretch out and press on toward the mark of the high calling of the Lord Jesus Christ." (Philippians 3:14.)

## 2. Total victory comes when we fully obey God's Word.

King Joash was given a word when Elisha said, "Take the arrow and strike the ground." The king hit the ground three times and stopped, but he was never told to stop; he should have kept hitting the ground over and over. But he didn't fully obey the word God had given him through Elisha. He didn't understand the importance of what he was doing.

Elisha's instructions must have seemed foolish to Joash. Think about it. If you were the king of Israel, and you were given an arrow and told to strike the ground, would that make any sense? Can you think of one good reason why you should be sitting in an old man's house hitting the ground with an arrow when your nation's business is waiting on you back at the palace?

So in an obligatory response to the man of God, Joash hits the ground a couple of times and then stops. But when he stops, he gets rebuked.

Let me tell you something about God's Word. When God gives us a word, it rarely makes sense to our carnal minds; in fact, it may seem downright foolish! But if God said it, it *always* works.

126

I'll give you an example. Let's say you are having financial problems, so you go to the Lord and ask for wisdom to solve your problems. Luke 6:38 says, **Give, and it shall be given unto you; good measure, pressed down, and shaken together, and running over, shall men give into your bosom** [or your lap]. That's giving to get more.

God gives seed to the sower and bread for food; He is able to make all grace abound to you, so that always having all sufficiency in all things, you will have an abundance for every good work. (2 Corinthians 9:8-10.)

This promise is given to those who sow seed. So you say, "God, I want more," and God says, "Good, then give it away." Now does that *ever* make sense?

But God's Word doesn't make sense to our carnal minds. So too many times we do as King Joash did and just "tap at the ground a few times." In other words, we say, "Okay, God, You're telling me to give, so I'll give." But we aren't really giving the way God says to give; we aren't willing to give as the widow gave her last mite. We should be sacrificially giving in obedience to God, believing that our act of faith, though it seems foolish and is given in secret, will cause a public victory.

Do you understand that every time the king struck the ground in private, it meant a public victory for God's people?

Do you understand that the little things done in private between yourself and God will create public victories and public testimonies? Do you realize that these little private acts of obedience are the basis of what God does in your life?

I have dealt with several pastors who fell during their ministry through immorality. Each of them, when describing their situation, said basically the same thing: "When I was in the ministry, I wasn't taking care of the details of my personal relationship with God before I fell. I wasn't praying or reading God's Word. I wasn't honest before God about my sins. I began to neglect those foundational elements in my life, and it led to my public failure."

The king of Israel was a public failure because he had been a private failure. He wouldn't do that which seemed insignificant and foolish to him.

I want you to understand that what God says to you is never insignificant and never foolish. **...I am not ashamed of the gospel of Christ: for it is the power of God unto salvation...** (Romans 1:16). It may be foolish to the world, but it is the power of God. When God speaks a word, it's never foolish.

You may say: "God, I want a promotion. I want the leaders of my church to recognize me. I want my boss at work to see the abilities I have in my life."

First Peter 5:6 says, **Humble yourselves therefore under the mighty hand of God, that he may exalt you** to raise **in due time** [or at the proper time]. James 4:6 says, **...God resisteth the proud, but giveth grace unto the humble.** God is saying, "If you want to be promoted, don't promote yourself; humble yourself and be the servant of all. I will exalt you at the proper time." Does this ever make sense? It makes more sense in the natural for us to promote ourselves — to go to someone and say, "I am incredibly gifted, but I've been overlooked. Can you do something about it?"

Here's what I have found about exalting or promoting yourself: Once you promote yourself into a position, you have to *keep* yourself in that position. If your flesh got you there, your flesh has to keep you there. You have to keep doing what the world does to get themselves into the positions they have achieved. That's when exhaustion or burnout comes.

But I realized a long time ago that God is my promoter. If God gets me there, He will keep me there. So I say: "Lord, I want to be humble; I want to be a servant. So I'm not promoting myself; I'm trusting You to get me where I'm going."

Now that may seem foolish in the eyes of the world, but that's God's way. Jesus spent thirty years in a carpenter's house before He began His ministry as the Messiah. During those years of humility and obscurity and of being overlooked, Jesus had to wait, wait, and wait. But He eventually fulfilled His divine purpose as the Messiah.

God knows when you are waiting. He knows what you are called to do. He knows what your time is and where your place is, and He is able to put you there. You just have to trust Him.

There are so many things the Bible says that simply don't make sense to the natural mind. And because they don't make sense, many times we don't do them or we just "tap" at them. But if we will aggressively do what God says to do and keep on doing it, we will see victory over and over again — in our marriages, in our finances, and in our ministries.

There is another issue related to totally obeying God's Word: Sometimes people simply refuse to obey it. Many people say they never hear God speaking to them; others say they just don't hear God's voice as they once did. They say, "At one time God spoke to me a lot, but He isn't speaking to me anymore."

If you haven't heard from God in a while, it may be that the last word He gave you hasn't been obeyed yet. Think about this: What did God say the last time He spoke to you? Did you do it?

Let me tell you about a situation I have dealt with many times as a pastor.

A husband comes to me and says, "My wife doesn't love me anymore. She's fed up with me. Our marriage is breaking up. What do I do?"

I share with him from Ephesians, chapter 5, and I say: "Your wife is offended because you've put work (or hunting, or fishing, or whatever) above her. As her husband, you are supposed to sacrifice your life for her, so go to her and repent. Then begin to nourish and cherish her."

When I say that to a husband, I can see the look on his face, and I know it's distasteful to him. But I tell him what the Word of God tells him to do anyway. So the husband leaves my office; then two or three months later, he comes back. His wife has left him, and they have gotten divorced. Now she is in love with another man. So he says, "What do I do now?"

In talking with him, I find that, after our first session, he didn't go to her and repent of all the things he had done and then really change his heart. Instead, like King Joash, he "tapped" a couple of times, saying, "Honey, I'm sorry; please come back." After doing that for two or three days, he thought, *Awww, she's gone. Just forget it!*

He was willing to "tap" for a while, but he wasn't willing to change his own ways. He wasn't willing to say: "God, I repent from my heart. Regardless of whether or not my wife ever believes me and returns, I'll never go back to a life of selfishness. I repent for living my life in carnality and compromise, and I commit myself totally to You and to Your Word."

Many people who are in desperate circumstances are just like those husbands I just talked about. They will only tap at the Word of God. They won't keep on doing it and doing it and doing it.

If God isn't speaking to you, what did you do the last time He spoke? If you haven't done what God has already told you to do, He will eventually stop speaking until you obey. Why should God continue speaking to an obstinate servant?

Reading the Bible isn't like walking down a cafeteria line and deciding what you would like to indulge in. You don't say, "Well, I like the Book of John, but I hate the Book of Leviticus" or "I love Matthew's gospel, but I hate the Book of Hebrews" or "I like this commandment, but I don't like that one." When you have the "cafeteria-line" mentality about God's Word, you are really saying, "I've made up my mind not to accept all that God says in His Word."

Suppose I have a problem, so I ask God, "What am I to do in the midst of this battle?" When God speaks, I may or may not do what He says. If I'm not totally sold out to do what He says, especially when it doesn't make sense, then He would say:

"Let Me tell you that I love you. It's My desire to speak into your life and to lead you into victory. But when you stiffen your neck against Me — when you scoff at what I say and just keep doing it your way — I won't speak to you about the situation again until you repent and are willing to completely obey Me.

"What did I say to you the last time, and what was your response? If you rejected My Word by scoffing at it and by continuing to do things your own way, I'm waiting for you to repent and to submit yourself to Me. When you're in trouble, come to Me. I will tell you what to do when you need to overcome a battle."

Total victory comes when we fully obey God's Word — when we do it and do it and do it, when we don't give up and we don't let go of its truth. Even though it doesn't seem to make sense, we have to strike the ground again and again and again — in our marriage, with our children, on the job, in our finances, with our ministry. Over and over again, we must do what God's Word says — and we must *never* give up! Then one day we will be able to look up and see that victory has come!

3. **Total victory comes when we totally commit ourselves to the battle.**

Let me tell you something about Joash: He wanted God to defeat the enemy *for* him but not *through* him. Remember Elisha's word to Joash: "Go and strike Syria until they are utterly defeated." (2 Kings 13:17.)

If you are praying for your marriage to work, but you aren't willing to be the vessel God would use to bring His love into your marriage, then you are wasting your prayers.

If you are praying for a family member, a neighbor, or a friend to be saved, but you aren't willing to be the instrument to share the Gospel with that person, then you are wasting your prayers.

If you are praying for physical healing, but you aren't willing to confess God's Word, to stand against the enemy, and to do whatever God says for you to do to participate in the victory, then you are wasting your prayers.

God has not called us to be eternal infants. He has called us to be kings and priests unto the Lord our God and co-heirs with Christ in His eternal kingdom.

When the Lord comes into our lives and we cry out to Him for victory, He asks us: "Will you be the warrior who stands up against the enemy? Will you be a participant in the battle? Be My voice to your wife or your husband. Love those who hate you. Pray for those who spitefully use you. Bless those who curse you. Stand up! Be an example. Be a witness. Be a prayer warrior. Be an intercessor."

Many times when we stand back and wonder why we didn't see the victory in a situation, it wasn't that God wouldn't come through for us; our defeat came because we wouldn't participate.

Jesus says, **I will give you the keys of the kingdom of heaven, and whatever you bind on earth will be bound in heaven....** (Matthew 16:19 NKJV). Can you imagine the enormity of Jesus' statement, "Whatever you bind..."?

He is actually saying: "What do you want to bind? I give *you* the keys to the kingdom of heaven. You're My Church, and the gates of hell cannot prevail against you. I have given you authority, so whatever you bind will be bound."

Are you binding anything? What do you want bound? You say, "I want the devil bound in my home." Then pray and bind him!

You see, you can cry to heaven and say: "God, I can feel the devil's breath on the back of my neck! Chase him off for me! He's taking my children. He's taking my home. He's taking our church, our city. Oh, God, woe is us!"

You are crying out to a merciful God. He loves you. He sent His only begotten Son to destroy the enemy and to take his foot off your neck. He has anointed you as the warrior who will overcome the enemy. But if you don't want the enemy in your life, you have to stand up and fight!

At one point in my life, I went through a time of real discouragement. Whenever I hear someone talking about depression, I can certainly understand, because I, too, went through a time when I was depressed and really feeling sorry for myself. It seemed that everything was coming against me. What I had worked so hard to build was being torn down, and I was watching it fall apart. It was as if Satan had thrown a heavy, cold blanket of darkness over me; I felt it physically. He was scoffing in my face at everything God had ever said to me.

God's blessing — that sense of light, life, peace, joy, happiness, and optimism He gives — had completely and totally left me. I found myself begging for death, as Elisha did after he was threatened by Jezebel: "God, take me out of here now; I can't put up with any more of this." (*See* 1 Kings 19:4.)

One day sitting in my office, I could feel that heavy oppression over me. I found myself praying, "Jesus, no

more pain. Please, Jesus, no more pain. Please help me."
Suddenly, I heard a voice and knew it was the voice of
my Savior. In my moment of need, He said, "You will
fight, or you will perish, Jimmy."

When I heard those words, my first response was,
"Lord, give me a break. Have You seen what I've been
through lately?" I wanted a word of comfort, a word
that just joined in with my self-pity and gave me the
sense that all of heaven was up there, feeling as sorry
for me as I was for myself.

Have you ever been so discouraged and felt so weak
that you just couldn't pray for yourself? The enemy
wants you to believe that there's nothing you can do
about it. He wants you to just keep sitting there, meditating on your problem and rehearsing it in your mind.
He wants you to lick your wounds and to nurse your
hurts, but never to pray.

But as I sat there and heard that word from God, I
knew it was right. An evil spirit had been attacking me
in my mind and in my body, but I began to pray. I said:
"I bind you, Satan, in the name of Jesus. I won't live
under your heel. I won't tolerate this depression any
longer." I just kept saying over and over, "I bind you, in
the name of Jesus. I bind you, in the name of Jesus."

Day after day, as I spoke that out in faith, I became
more and more encouraged. Every time I said that to
the devil, I was empowered even more to say it the next
time.

After a few weeks had gone by, I no longer felt hopeless and helpless under that heavy blanket of oppression. Instead, I was literally standing over the enemy in
the Spirit realm, pronouncing his curse and his demise.
I'd say with absolute conviction:

"I bind you, Satan, in the name of Jesus Christ! We
will not let a spirit of depression or rebellion into this
family. We will not allow a lying spirit or faultfinding

spirit into this church. The blood of Jesus is against you, Satan. You have no place over my mind or my body, over our children or our finances, over this church or this city. We bind you, in Jesus' name!"

Jesus is saying to us: "Grow up. Be a man of God [or a woman] of God. After you are saved and receive the Baptism of the Holy Spirit, I'll carry you for a while. But there comes a point when I set you down on *your* feet and make you start to walk. I do that not because I don't love you or don't understand what you're going through, but because I want you to experience the victory with Me of seeing Satan fall from heaven like lightning."

In Luke 10, when the seventy disciples returned to Jesus after healing the sick, raising the dead and preaching the Gospel, Jesus said to them, **...I saw Satan fall like lightning from heaven** (Luke 10:18 NKJV).

That's the thrill of overcoming the enemy — of standing up against the forces of hell that have come to destroy us and then watching them flee. It's exhilarating!

4. **Total victory comes when we decide we won't accept anything less.**

This doesn't mean that we grumble or have an unthankful spirit or a lack of contentment for where we are in life right now. It means that we have made the decision not to live in compromise.

We are to press forward toward the mark that God has set for us, and we are to never allow compromise to come into our lives.

Do you want victory? Are you willing to live in anything less? Have you given up on what God told you in the past? Have you compromised on the vision He put in your heart because the devil told you that it can't happen through you, that you're inadequate for the task? Don't compromise! Remember, Joash was only three strikes away from total victory.

Did you know that shortly before David became king of Israel, his family was stolen from him, and the people who had faithfully followed him were talking about stoning him? He was at the bottom rung of his life.

Then it says, **...But David strengthened himself in the Lord his God** (1 Samuel 30:6 NKJV). As a result, David was able to regain the support of his men so they could chase the enemy and recover all that had been stolen from them. And in the next chapter of David's life, he became king.

You may be discouraged right now, but in the next chapter of your life, you will see the vision. So, don't give up. Don't surrender. Don't accept anything less than total victory!

God has given you an anointed Word, and He will give you an anointed weapon for every battle you have to face if you will seek Him and find out what that weapon is. He has made you an anointed warrior, and He has put the arrows in your hand — arrows that the world calls foolish, arrows that may seem insignificant. It's up to you to take those arrows and strike the ground — and don't stop striking until you see the victory! Be zealous. Be faithful. Be hot for Christ. And never give up — *never* give up!

# 6

# *GOD'S PERSON THROUGH*

# *GOD'S PROCESS*

*To become God's <u>person</u>, we have to go through God's <u>process.</u> And God's process isn't always easy. God is the Potter, and we are the clay. He is always working on us, always shaping us, always molding us. He loves us so much that He works on some of us overtime in order to shape us His way.*

*If you're ever going to become a perfect vessel of honor to be used by God, or in other words, the person God wants you to be — <u>you</u> have to be taken through a certain process. Even though at times God will allow us to go through difficult situations in life, He does it because He loves us.*

**— Tim Storey**

6

## *GOD'S PERSON THROUGH GOD'S PROCESS*

### by Tim Storey
*Tim Storey Ministries*
*La Mirada, California*

I want to talk to you about how we become God's person through God's process. Let's begin by looking at Ephesians 4:1,2 NIV:

**As a prisoner for the Lord, then, I urge you to live a life worthy of the calling you have received. Be completely humble and gentle; be patient, bearing with one another in love.**

Then in verses 11-13 NIV, it says:

**It was he who gave some to be apostles, some to be prophets, some to be evangelists, and some to be pastors and teachers, to prepare God's people for works of service, so that the body of Christ may be built up until we all reach unity in the faith and in the knowledge of the Son of God and become mature, attaining to the whole measure of the fullness of Christ.**

In verse 1, the apostle Paul says that you have been called.

Let me say, first of all, that I appreciate what I heard my good friend, Benny Hinn, say one time: that all of us have been called in this last move of God. It isn't just going to be a few pastors, or a few evangelists, or a few prophets. I believe God is calling the whole team.

139

### A *God* Idea

The Greek word for "called" is the word *Klesis,*[*] which means "to be called out to a specific purpose." I want you to realize that you have been called to a specific purpose.

Now, there is what I would call a *good* idea for our lives and there is a *God* idea. Good ideas *may* come true, but God ideas *must* come true. There are more than seven thousand prophecies in the Bible, and I know that one of them has to be for you. Proverbs 3:5,6 NKJV says:

**Trust in the Lord with all your heart, and lean not on your own understanding;**

**In all your ways acknowledge Him, and He shall direct your paths.**

The Bible says a righteous man's steps are ordered by the Lord. (Psalm 37:23.) That means God has a specific plan for your life. That's a God idea, not a good idea.

Most people are walking in what they perceive are "good" ideas. They say, "Well, this would be a good person to marry," or, "That would be a good ministry to get involved with."

But I believe that God has called you out for a specific purpose, and that purpose is a God idea. Again, I tell you that good ideas may come true, but God ideas must come true. What I want is for you to discover the God idea for your life.

### Calling and Character

Notice once more what the apostle Paul says in Ephesians 4:1,2 NIV:

**As a prisoner for the Lord, then, I urge you to live a life worthy of the calling you have received. Be completely**

---

[*] *Vine's Complete Expository Dictionary of Old and New Testament Words* (Nashville/Atlanta/London/Vancouver), p. 86.

**humble and gentle; be patient, bearing with one another in love.**

First of all, Paul talks about the calling we have received. We all like it when people tell us good things about our lives and about our future. Well, Paul says you have been called by God. But then he goes on to say that you must be humble, patient, and gentle; he begins to talk about the fruits of the Spirit.

Now there is a difference between *calling* and *character*. Many people have a great calling, but they have no character. They are visionary heavyweights but character lightweights.

God wants us to have a powerful calling *and* a powerful character. So after He calls us, He begins to train us.

In 1988, many of my good friends began to tell me: "We're going to have a great revival because God has to move in a forty-year cycle. In 1906 to 1908, there was the Azusa Street revival; then in 1948, the great healing revival came with the Voice of Healing. So in 1988, there will be another powerful revival."

But instead of revival in 1988, the Church experienced some major trials and tribulations.

I remember that when I was in school, from time to time the teachers would give us a little quiz to find out if we had been doing our homework. We were supposed to read a certain number of chapters a day, so they would give us what they called a "pop quiz." They wouldn't tell us in advance; they would just surprise us with a test. When a pop quiz was announced, I would always get really nervous if I hadn't done my homework or my reading.

That's what God did to the Body of Christ in 1988: When we were ready for a great move of God, He gave us a pop quiz instead. God's two-part quiz question was, "Are you able to endure revivals, tribulations and trials?

Are you walking in the truly tested character of My chosen and called?"

Then the trials began to come, and the Body of Christ began to fail. Most of the churches began to decline. Pastors were arguing with each other. People were murmuring and complaining. We had the calling, but God has to build His character in us.

### Becoming God's Person
### by Going Through God's Process

In order to become God's person, you have to go through God's process. And God's process isn't always easy. I like what Billy Graham has said: "God loves you just the way you are, but He loves you too much to leave you the same."

So guess what? God is always working on us. He is always shaping us, always molding us. He loves us so much that He works on some of us overtime to mold us into His image.

I will never forget one day in Bible school. I had been reading books by some great men of God, so on this particular day I got excited and decided that I would become a powerful man of God like those I had read about.

I went into the chapel where prayer was held at certain times. It was 10:00 o'clock at night and I couldn't find any anointing oil, so I got some cooking oil and put it on my hands. As a young man on fire for God, I lifted up my hands and said, "God, whether You or me, or anyone else likes it or not, I will be used in a powerful way. Every morning I'll be here in this chapel seeking You, because I'm going to be a powerful evangelist."

Now I know God heard my prayers because the Bible says He does. But all of a sudden, trials and tests and tribulations began to come into my life. Why? Because diverse temptations and the testing of our faith produce endurance. (James 1:2,3.) And because God said, "Okay, so you want to be called? Then let's build your character." If I was going to become God's person, I had to go through God's process.

## The Potter and the Clay

In Jeremiah, chapter 18, we find this story:

**This is the word that came to Jeremiah from the Lord: "Go down to the potter's house, and there I will give you my message." So I went down to the potter's house, and I saw him working at the wheel. But the pot he was shaping from the clay was marred in his hands; so the potter formed it into another pot, shaping it as seemed best to him.**

**Jeremiah 18:1-4** NIV

I want you to realize that God is the Potter and you are the clay. You have to get that down in your spirit. Problems arise in your life when you live by what I call the "Frank Sinatra theology": You want to do it *your way*.

So as the Potter, God has a plan for your life. He wants to shape you the way that seems best to Him — the *God* idea, not the *good* idea.

In Jeremiah 18:5,6 NIV, it goes on to say:

**Then the word of the Lord came to me: "O house of Israel, can I not do with you as this potter does?" declares the Lord. "Like clay in the hand of the potter, so are you in my hand, O house of Israel."**

If you're ever going to become a perfect vessel of honor to be used by God — in other words, the person God wants *you* to be — you have to be taken through a certain process. That is God's job.

Even though at times God allows us to go through difficult situations in life, He does it because He loves us.

Let me give you an illustration. When a military commander is getting his troops ready for battle, he won't always act lovingly towards them. For instance, that commander doesn't come to those young soldiers at five in the morning and sweetly say: "Now a lot of us will be running about five miles this morning, but you don't have to come along if you don't want to. If you boys are a little sleepy, just stay in bed. If you'd like some breakfast, we can make you some bacon and eggs."

That will never happen! It's the job of the military officer to get his soldiers prepared. He always sounds tough when he talks to them. He tells the soldiers, "All right, move it! Move it! Move it! Move it!" Why? Because he has to get them ready for battle.

Well, the same is true with us. We are always preaching and singing about who we are in God and about our victory in Jesus. We are always proclaiming that as the Joshua generation, we are going to win. So God says to us, "Okay — then get up! Move it! Move it! Move it!" We complain, "But I don't like that!" Then He says, "Well, you asked for it, and you got it!"

You see, you become God's person through God's process. You are the one who asked to be trained for battle.

So God is the Potter, and you are the clay. You sit there, and He works on you. That's how it goes. He's smarter than you, and He knows the past, the present, and the future.

According to one psychologist, we use about 10 percent of our brain. So here we are, trying to figure out an all-knowing God with only 10 percent of our brain! We just need to be the clay and let God be the Potter. Remember, that's what God is trying to be in our lives.

## Steps To Becoming a Vessel of Honor

There are certain steps that a potter must go through in working the clay in order for it to eventually become a vessel of honor. Let's look at these steps.

The first step the potter takes when making a pot is to dig dirt from the ground. That's what Jesus did to us. The Bible says that Jesus became sin for us who knew no sin that we might be made the righteousness of God. (2 Corinthians 5:21.) He took us out of iniquity, and we became righteous.

The second step the potter takes in this process is to soak the dirt that he's removed from the ground in water. The potter pours water all over the clay until it is soaked through and through.

The third step the potter takes is to smite the clay and work it thoroughly. He begins to work that dirt as he molds it and molds it and molds it. That's how some Christians feel: as if they are being worked by the Potter's hands over and over again.

Now, God gives us the promise of great things, and He gives the principles. But after the promise and the principles, we always have to confront the problems. But we don't like to hear preaching about the problems; we like to hear about all the promises.

First, you receive the promise. Then you obey the principles or the conditions, which basically means living according to the Word of God. Next you have to overcome the problems. Finally, you obtain prosperity, or that which was promised.

So first you are dug out of the ground, or taken out of sin. Then you get soaked with water, which is the Holy Spirit coming on you.

Next comes the third step: He begins to thoroughly work the clay, which is you! In other words, He allows tests and trials to come into your life so that you will become more mature; you will become like shining gold, a worthy vessel of honor. That's why God allows this process of the promise, the principles, and the problems to take place.

It's in this problem stage where a lot of us get mad. We say, "God, I don't understand what's happening. I just went to a Bible conference, and now I'm going through all these trials." Well, you asked to be used of God. He's just doing His job of allowing you to be trained and molded and shaped.

You see, we like the promise stage. We like to hear things that talk about who we are in Christ and that we are the head and not the tail, above and not beneath, going over and not under.

We love those promises. We love those principles. But there will always be problems.

Sometimes it isn't the devil who causes all the problems in your life. Sometimes God allows difficult situations to come because He loves you enough to build character in you. In those cases, you'd just be wasting your time to bind and rebuke the devil.

So in God's process, the clay is dug from the ground and soaked in water (the power of the Holy Spirit). Then God begins to work you thoroughly because He loves you so much.

I once watched a potter as he worked the clay to make a pot. He kept pushing that lumpy clay to the center of the wheel. But as he worked the clay, it seemed to be fighting him. The potter had to stay focused on what he was doing in order to keep the clay in the center of the wheel.

That is often how God disciplines you. Sometimes when He has His hands on you — when He is working you, positioning you into the center of His will through discipline — you may say, "Where are You, God?" But He's always right there, saying, "I'm looking right at you!"

So God begins to push you to the center of the wheel — His will — because you asked for it: You said that you wanted to be mighty; you wanted to be part of God's victorious army.

As God pushes you along in life, you might say, "Ohhh, God is working me too hard. Ohhh, I feel another trial coming." But God keeps telling you, "I'm shaping you because I love you."

So God puts you in the center of the wheel and begins to work on you. He really concentrates as He shapes you. He works on you the way that potter I watched worked that lump of clay, pulling and pushing and molding that clay until he had shaped it into a beautiful pot.

Now after we've been worked on for a while and things get a little easier, we might think that the process is all over. We begin to see ourselves as victorious, and we start confessing, "I'm the head and not the tail. I'm above and not beneath. I'm going over now!"

This is the stage in God's process when preachers may be seen walking around at conferences all full of pride, passing out business cards and calling themselves "Bishop" or "Doctor." But God looks at His children and says, "I'm not done with you; there are three more steps to go."

The next step takes place after the pot is formed but is still wet. At this point, most potters will take a thin wire and begin to push it through the clay. They are investigating the clay for air bubbles. That's a picture of the Holy Spirit searching your heart to check your motives.

*So you want to be anointed?*

*So you want to be another Oral Roberts?*

*So you want to preach like Dr. Morris Cerullo?*

When that thin wire goes through you, you say, "Ooooh! Ahhhh! Ohhhh! That one really hurt!"

Maybe you want to be anointed like Benny Hinn. I have been close to Benny Hinn for more than ten years. I have seen what he has gone through in order to flow in ministry the way he does.

Should you have that kind of anointing without strong, godly character? God says no, so He takes that thin wire and begins to investigate your life for "air bubbles." He most often uses other people to do it, and many times they are people you don't like.

So you were feeling good for a while — until you got all bloated up with pride. Then that Holy Ghost "wire" went to work in your life. That's when God began to check your heart for the smallest of wrong motives. (We can't even get away with gossiping in the '90s!) And it wasn't long before all those bloated-up "pride bubbles" started bursting!

After the potter finishes checking for air bubbles, he begins to mold and to shape the pot again. Finally, he has a pot that has been nicely molded back into shape again.

So now you are feeling good again. You have been molded, shaped, and checked for wrong motives, and you're looking like a good pot. This is the stage in the process when you feel that you are ready to go out and touch your world, whatever your profession or calling is. But there are still a couple of stages left in the process. This is the interesting part — what this message is all about.

## The Patience Test

At this point, God grabs you, and you think He's about to take you out into the limelight — you are headed for the big time! But something else takes place instead:

The potter takes the molded pot, puts it up on a shelf, and leaves it there to dry and to harden. When this takes place in your life, it's called the "patience test."

That's Jesus, living in His hometown for thirty years and then ministering for only three.

That's the apostle Paul, living thirteen years in the wilderness.

That's Moses, living in the wilderness for forty years and asking, "God, where have You been?"

We don't like the patience test, do we? We like everything to come to us fast. We want our hamburgers cooked fast; we want our hair styled fast. We want everything fast. But God doesn't work that way. In order for us to become the person God wants us to be, we must go through God's process.

So God puts you up on that shelf. He places you there to allow you to cool down just a little bit so that the character qualities He has molded and shaped in you can set permanently. And that's when you start getting nervous.

There are three things that can happen while we are up there on that shelf.

## "Shouting From the Shelf"

First of all, we may begin to do what I call "shouting from the shelf." That's something that can be found in most churches. Some may call it worrying, backbiting, and complaining.

Shouting from the shelf can occur when a sister thinks she ought to be singing in the choir, but the pastor won't let her. Sitting there on the shelf, she may complain, "I don't know why he won't let me sing. I'm a great soloist."

Shouting from the shelf occurs when a young preacher says, "I don't know who they think Tim Storey is. I don't think he's so great. Why don't they let *me* preach? I could really bless them!"

You're shouting from the shelf when you say, "I don't know why that sister is getting blessed. I know how she has lived her life. I'm supposed to get the hundredfold. What's going on?"

God put you on the shelf, and now you have begun to shout and to complain. And God dislikes it. The longer you shout from the shelf, the more God will just let you stay there.

## Prophesying to One Another

The second thing that often happens during the patience test in many Christian circles is that brothers and sisters in the Lord begin to prophesy to one another.

For instance, suppose you see a brother who looks like he is really going through a tough time. (As I mentioned earlier, we always want to say that our problems are caused by the devil, but sometimes God has been working overtime in a person's life.)

You love to prophesy, so you say to that brother: "Thus saith the Lord: You're going to be used in a mighty way — so mighty that I can't even tell you how mighty it is." Then that person tries hard to get down off the shelf to go do those mighty exploits. But all the time God is telling him, "Get back on that shelf!"

When someone comes to you and says, "I see something in the Spirit," maybe you have been on that shelf for so long that you're willing to see anything. All you want is to get down off that shelf!

People like to prophesy to one another, because they want to get each other off that shelf. They say, "Oh, you don't need to go through that, Brother," so they start prophesying to one another.

You see, that's what so many Christians do in our churches today. God has allowed some churches to be on the shelf. But then men and women of God come into those churches and start prophesying: "Thus saith the Lord, this church will turn this city around for God!" But nothing happens. Why? Because that was a good idea, but it wasn't a God idea. That's why so many of God's people are so frustrated.

Suppose someone came to you with a good idea, saying you were going to be rich and famous and live in Hollywood. But it didn't happen, so now you're mad at God. That may have been a *good* idea, but not a *God* idea. Maybe what was prophesied to you was not of God.

### Doing It Our Own Way

The third thing we often do when we're going through the patience test is to decide to get off the shelf ourselves and do things our own way. While sitting on the shelf, we begin to have such thoughts as:

*I'm tired of sitting on this shelf. If I have to start my own ministry, I'll do it.*

*I'm tired of sitting on this shelf. I don't want to follow that pastor anymore. I'll just start my own church.*

*I'm tired of sitting on this shelf. I've had the same wife for thirty years, so I'm going to find myself a new wife.*

There are many Christians who have decided to do things their own way. They have gotten down off the shelf and are looking for a good idea, saying, "I have to find that good idea for my life. Where did it go?"

But God is still back there on that shelf, and He has the God idea. So if we want to discover the God idea for our lives, we can't get off the shelf until God comes and takes us down.

### The Final Steps

God usually doesn't take you off the shelf until you are tired and wondering if you even want to get off the shelf. Then He comes and gets you.

When God pulls you off the shelf, you say, "I'm sure glad I'm going somewhere. I have no idea where I'm going, but it must be the will of God."

So you have gone through all the steps of God's process that we've discussed so far. You were dug from the ground, soaked in water, and worked over thoroughly. During the process, God concentrated on shaping you and pushing you to the center of His will. Then that Holy Ghost wire went through you so that corrections and adjustments could be made. Finally, you were put up on the shelf, and you just stayed there, waiting until God was ready to use you. You didn't move around anywhere, because you weren't following your own will; you submitted your will to God's will.

Now the next step the potter takes is to cover the pot with glaze. It makes the pot look special when it is given such a shiny coat.

At this stage in God's process, you don't know what's happening; you just feel as if something is going on with you. You say, "I guess God is still preparing me."

In the last step of the process, the potter places the pot in the furnace.

When the Potter grabs you and puts you in the furnace, you sit down next to the rest of us pots. We look at each other as if to say, "You've been through it too, huh? Well, let the healing begin."

While we're all in the furnace, God says, "These are My children; I made them. They can take it hotter than that. Turn up the heat!"

At this final stage, if you haven't gone through every single step, you will do one of two things: you will either crack, or you will explode. But if you went through every step of the process that the Potter wanted you to endure, you will eventually come out of the furnace, shining brightly with the "glaze" of spiritual maturity, and you will make it through to the end.

I know what it's like to be pressed. I know what it's like to have that wire go through you. I know what it's like to be on the shelf for a long time. But I also know what it was like when Father God came and took me down. Take my word for it — it's worth the wait!

I want you to realize that God is in the process of shaping your life. So, don't crack or explode. Be strong. Go through every step in God's process. Remember, the Potter is in control!

I like a line from an old song that says, "It will be worth it all when we see Jesus." Just thank the Lord that He is in control of your life. Thank Him and praise Him in the midst of the trials and tests that come your way, knowing that when the Potter has completed His work, He will bring you forth as **...a vessel for honor, sanctified and useful for the Master, prepared for every good work** (2 Timothy 2:21 NKJV).

# 7

# *WALK IN BOLDNESS*

*I have good news for you: If you're a child of God, you can be bold in Jesus Christ! The Greater One dwells within you.*

*The highest, greatest, and most anointed way to be a witness for Jesus is to let people see the reality of the Resurrection in <u>you</u> and <u>through</u> you.*

**— Ray McCauley**

7

## *WALK IN BOLDNESS*

### by Ray McCauley
*Pastor, Rhema Bible Church*
*Randburg, South Africa*

In dealing with the subject of boldness, we will look first at how we can have boldness. Then we will see how to walk in boldness.

In our walk with God, we have to be bold. We have to reach out and begin to let God work through us as we minister to others.

One night as my wife and I were leaving a restaurant, there were some young people standing outside with a guitar. Right beside the restaurant was a bar, and those kids were just praising and worshipping God. I stood there for a bit; then I started praising and worshipping God along with them. It really thrilled my heart to see young people who had the guts, the boldness, to do something like that for God.

Acts 4:13 NKJV is one of my favorite Scriptures:

**Now when they saw the boldness of Peter and John, and perceived that they were uneducated and untrained men, they marveled. And they realized that they had been with Jesus.**

Notice that this verse *doesn't* say, "Now when they saw the boldness of Peter and John, they perceived that they were theologians with many years of training."

It's amazing how some people react when we start to reach out to others and share what God has placed within our hearts. Immediately they say, "Who do you think you are? You haven't had the right education. You haven't been trained up in the right way."

I see nothing wrong with going to Bible school or receiving theological training to learn the Word of God. The Body of Christ needs that.

But you don't have to be educated to be used of God. You don't need *ability*; you firstly need *availability*. God will take whatever you present to Him and use it for His glory.

It goes on in Acts 4:29,30 NKJV to say this:

**"Now, Lord, look on their threats, and grant to Your servants that with all boldness they may speak Your word, by stretching out Your hand to heal, and that signs and wonders may be done through the name of Your holy Servant Jesus."**

Then verse 31 NKJV says:

**And when they had prayed....**

It's scriptural for us to pray and ask God to give us a boldness that we have never had before. But many times we get intimidated; we feel so insecure in our desire to reach out to people that we never fulfill what God wants to do through us. We find ourselves not being obedient to how God wants to use us for His glory.

Continuing in Acts 4:31 NKJV it says:

**And when they had prayed, the place where they were assembled together was shaken; and they were all filled with the Holy Spirit, and they spoke the word of God with boldness.**

In Acts 2:4, it says the believers that were praying together in the upper room were all filled with the Holy Ghost. Then here, just two chapters later, we see that many of these same believers were all filled with the Holy Spirit.

Does that mean they had to get filled again in order to receive the fullness of the Holy Spirit? No. But every Christian who is Spirit-filled, or baptized in the Holy Spirit, needs a continual fresh touch of the Holy Ghost — a continual anointing of God's Spirit — to flow through them.

The biggest problem with certain people, particularly Charismatics and Pentecostals, is that they will come to you and say, "Do you remember what God did back in 1956?" They can always tell you what God did years ago, but they can't tell you what He did last month! They are still living in the past rather than in the present.

God doesn't live in the past; He doesn't even live in the future — He lives in the *now!* And all of us need a refreshing, a fresh touch, an anointing of God. We need God to fill us. So we should pray daily, "God, just fill me with Your Holy Spirit; let the fresh oil of Your anointing flow."

**And with great power the apostles gave witness to the resurrection of the Lord Jesus. And great grace was upon them all.**

**Acts 4:33 NKJV**

A witness is someone who testifies to something that's true. If a person goes to court as a witness, he testifies that what he is saying is true. So in Acts 4:33, these people who were witnesses had proof — God's anointing and power in their lives — that there is a resurrected Christ Who is alive.

The highest, greatest, and most anointed way to be a witness for Jesus is to let people see the reality of the Resurrection *in* you and *through* you.

## Be Bold as a Lion

**The wicked flee when no one pursues, But the righteous are bold as a lion.**

**Proverbs 28:1** NKJV

Praise God, we can have boldness — we can be bold as a lion!

One night at our church, a man who was involved in the satanic church came to hinder or break up our service. But all of a sudden during the service, without any prompting or anyone knowing anything about the man, we all began to pray in the Spirit. As we prayed, the man jumped up and ran out of the church.

Thank God, the people at our church are bold, so some of our men went after the man and brought him back inside. That night he came down front and received the Lord Jesus.

Some people think that the devil has all power and all authority, that he is so great and God is so small. They are terrified of demonic manifestations.

But I have good news for you: If you're a child of God, you can be bold in Jesus Christ! The Greater One dwells within you. Greater is He that's in you than he that is in the world! (1 John 4:4.)

Now let's look at three areas in which you can be bold.

### Boldness Towards Heaven

First, you are to be *bold towards heaven*. Now I'm not talking here about arrogance. You don't ever boss God around, not anywhere, not any time. If you try to do that, you will find yourself in trouble quickly, and you will wish you had never done it.

But there is a boldness you can have in your relationship with God. You can talk to God as if you are talking to your earthly father. And you can do it without sounding Elizabethan! Hebrews 4:16 NKJV says:

160

**Let us therefore come boldly to the throne of grace, that we may obtain mercy and find grace to help in time of need.**

You can go to your heavenly Father in boldness, by the Word of God and by the anointing of God. You can enter into His Holy Place, into the Holy of Holies, through the blood of Jesus. You can come into His very presence in right standing, washed and cleansed in His blood. When God looks upon you, He doesn't see your old sinful nature; He sees the blood of Jesus that has cleansed you and washed away your sins.

Don't listen to the devil. He will try to convince you that you will never be worthy of God, putting thoughts in your mind such as: *How can you stand up and say you're a child of God when you've had a past like yours and you've had so many problems?*

Look at Hebrews 10:19 NKJV. This will change your prayer life! It says:

**Therefore, brethren, having boldness to enter the Holiest** [the Holy Place] **by the blood of Jesus.**

You can come into the Holy Place twenty-four hours a day — through His blood!

Did you know that every time you say, "In the name of Jesus," and speak to God, you are praying? That's what prayer is: communicating with God.

Some people think it's sacrilegious if you talk to God while driving along in your motorcar. But you can talk to Him in the bathtub or the shower. You can communicate with God wherever you go.

You can come boldly into the throne room of God, into the very presence of God, because you are in right standing with Him. Second Corinthians 5:21 NKJV says, **For He made Him who knew no sin to be sin for us, that we might become the righteousness of God in Him.**

161

Isn't that wonderful? You have been made righteous. You are a child of God, a priest, a king, an ambassador.

But you have to be bold and act out what has been placed within you. You can't just say, "Hallelujah, I'm righteous," and act any way you want. If you are in right-standing with God, you have to *live* like it.

It's important to understand the character of God. Look at Jeremiah 9:23,24 NKJV:

**Thus says the Lord: "Let not the wise man glory in his wisdom, Let not the mighty man glory in his might, Nor let the rich man glory in his riches;**

**"But let him who glories glory in this, That he understands and knows Me, That I am the Lord, exercising lovingkindness, judgment, and righteousness in the earth. For in these I delight," says the Lord.**

Psalm 145 describes God this way:

**The Lord is gracious and full of compassion, Slow to anger and great in mercy.**

**The Lord is good to all, And His tender mercies are over all His works.**

**All Your works shall praise You, O Lord, And Your saints shall bless You.**

**They shall speak of the glory of Your kingdom, And talk of Your power,**

**To make known to the sons of men His mighty acts, And the glorious majesty of His kingdom.**

**Your kingdom is an everlasting kingdom, And Your dominion endures throughout all generations.**

**Psalm 145:8-13** NKJV

You may say, "Well, if God's dominion endures throughout all generations, how come we don't see enough of it?"

Someone once complained to the German evangelist Reinhard Bonnke: "The blood! The blood! The blood! You keep talking about the blood of Jesus! If the blood of Jesus were so powerful, then why are things on the earth so bad?" Reinhard replied, "You know, you can work in a soap factory and stink. But until you take that soap and apply it by washing your body, it won't do you any good!"

The blood of Jesus is available to every human being who will say: "Jesus Christ, I accept You as my Lord and Savior. I accept that Your blood was shed for me. I turn from my way now to follow You, because I receive You as Lord and make You the Lord of my life."

Once you have made this decision from your heart, the blood of Jesus goes into operation. And no demon can stop you from being born again, from being washed in the blood of Jesus, from being placed in right standing with God. If the devil were all that powerful and mighty, don't you think he would have prevented that miracle from taking place in your life?

## Boldness Towards Hell

You can be *bold towards hell.* We always hear about what the devil is doing. But let me tell you, the devil is no match for God.

At a meeting one night, a man in the salvation line jumped forward and tried to choke me. I cried, "Jesus!" and the man fell to the ground as stiff as a plank, unconscious. The ushers picked him up and carried him out. Thirty minutes later, he woke up and was led to the Lord.

Do you believe God's Word that says greater is He that is in you than he that is in the world? (1 John 4:4.) Do you believe that you have authority over witchcraft, over demons, over principalities and powers? You don't have to find some minister to bind the devil's works — *you* have that authority through Jesus!

Every man who is a child of God has spiritual authority over his home. So, men, take that authority!

Imagine this: As head of your house, you are sitting at home one night when suddenly some guy walks through the door and starts smashing up everything he can find. He kicks in your TV and tears up your kitchen; then he walks out to your car and starts splashing it with paint. Would you just sit there thinking, *Well, whatever will be will be. Maybe God is testing me?* No! You would stand up against that intruder and fight to protect your home!

Whenever sickness, disease, fear, or anything else from the devil comes knocking at your door, you can be bold to stand against it in Jesus' name. Then when your faith opens that door, you won't find anything there!

So you can be bold towards hell!

**Then He called His twelve disciples together and gave them power and authority over all demons, and to cure diseases.**

**Luke 9:1 NKJV**

Jesus gave the disciples power *and* authority! Did you know that if you operate in authority, you don't need power; and if you operate in power, you don't need authority?

Picture this: A traffic policeman is standing at an intersection. A ten-ton truck so powerful that it could just squash him flat comes rolling toward him.

All the policeman has to do is lift his arm into the air, and the truck driver will put on the brakes and stop. Why? Because the policeman has been given authority by his police department, and that entire department will back him up.

You can have boldness in God because you have been given power *and* authority. You have the power of the Holy Spirit at your disposal. You have the name of Jesus and the blood of Jesus. And heaven will back you up!

Having disarmed principalities and powers, He made a public spectacle of them, triumphing over them in it.

*Colossians 2:15 NKJV*

Then the seventy returned with joy, saying, "Lord, even the demons are subject to us in Your name."

And He said to them, "I saw Satan fall like lightning from heaven.

"Behold, I give you the authority to trample on serpents and scorpions, and over all the power of the enemy, and nothing shall by any means hurt you.

"Nevertheless do not rejoice in this, that the spirits are subject to you, but rather rejoice because your names are written in heaven."

*Luke 10:17-20 NKJV*

What if God had to choose whether it was more important for you to cast out demons or to go to heaven? (Now of course, this isn't a choice that God will ever have to make.) But if God ever did have to choose, He would say that it is more important for you to go to heaven.

If you ask God which is more important, physical healing or salvation for eternity, His answer in a split second would be salvation.

Everybody is always looking for miracles, but when you see people come to the front of the church and receive Jesus Christ as Lord and Savior, that's the greatest miracle there could ever be.

## Boldness Towards Earth

We should all be *bold towards earth* — in other words, bold to witness to others about Jesus. One of our greatest problems is that we're the silent majority. It's time that we Christians arise as God's army and bust up the devil's works in this world, such as racism and humanism and atheism!

It's time for us to stand up and to declare that Jesus Christ is alive and real. We can't just sit around all the time, playing dead.

I was so thrilled the night I saw all those youngsters standing outside the restaurant that was next door to a bar, singing and praising and worshipping God. It's about time our youngsters got stirred up enough to go out and challenge the devil right where he is!

Someone might ask those young people, "What right have you to stand there, praising God?"

They have all the right in the world. And it's about time the rest of us started being bold like that. We're here to enforce Satan's defeat. What right does he have to put our kids on drugs, to get them drunk, or to cause them to go crazy and shoot at each other or cut each other to pieces?

**"You are the salt of the earth; but if the salt loses its flavor, how shall it be seasoned? It is then good for nothing but to be thrown out and trampled underfoot by men.**

**"You are the light of the world. A city that is set on a hill cannot be hidden.**

**"Nor do they light a lamp and put it under a basket, but on a lampstand, and it gives light to all who are in the house.**

**"Let your light so shine before men, that they may see your good works and glorify your Father in heaven."**

**Matthew 5:13-16 NKJV**

There is not one Scripture that can be found — except maybe in "the Book of First Imaginations"— that says, "My belief is personal; it's between me and God." Think about that.

You know, as a Christian, you should be like the chicken pox. If you really have the light and life of God in you, you can't help but spread it around! When you are full of God, when you have the light and life of Jesus in you, people will see it. Some of them may not be too happy about it, but just let your light shine anyway. Be bold about it.

Born-again believers have absolutely nothing to be ashamed of. I'm not embarrassed about the fact that I love God, and I'm not afraid to be a witness for Jesus. But people have complained to me about my boldness.

One day I was talking to a pharmacist, who said, "How dare your people stand by the supermarket and preach! If I want to hear what they have to say, I'll go to them; they don't have to come to me."

But when you have something that's so real and has been such a blessing and a reality in your life, you want everybody to have it, especially those you love. That's why you witness. Not only that, but you also believe there is a heaven and a hell.

**But when He** [Jesus] **saw the multitudes, He was moved with compassion for them, because they were weary and scattered, like sheep having no shepherd.**

**Then He said to His disciples, "The harvest truly is plentiful, but the laborers are few. Therefore pray the Lord of the harvest to send out laborers into His harvest."**

**Matthew 9:36-38 NKJV**

Our problem is not finding a harvest; our problem is finding laborers to bring in the harvest! There are many, many people in the world today who are ripe, who will listen and respond to Jesus. There are even people who don't like church, but will respond to Jesus.

If we will just start being bold to stand up and declare what God has provided for us and what He wants to do in our lives, I believe we can turn entire nations around.

Then God can have His complete way as we submit our lives.

## Living a Life of Boldness

Now I want to continue on the subject of boldness by looking at some practical ways of walking in a life of boldness. Boldness is daring to declare God's Word and what we believe is right.

Here is one of the greatest definitions I have ever heard for the word *compromise:* to accept what you don't believe because you refuse to fight for what you do believe.

So one facet of being bold in God is to become strong and willing to declare the truth. But another aspect of boldness has to do with accepting our healing.

There will be times when we have to fight symptoms that attack our bodies. You see, if divine healing is in the Word of God, then we must be bold to declare God's Word concerning that situation and be willing to fight for it. Did you know that Christianity is actually a fight? Look at what the Scriptures say:

**Fight the good fight of faith....**

**1 Timothy 6:12**

**Put on the whole armour of God, that ye may be able to stand against the wiles of the devil.**

**For we wrestle not against flesh and blood, but against principalities, against powers, against the rulers of the darkness of this world, against spiritual wickedness in high places.**

**Ephesians 6:11,12**

*Every* believer needs to walk in boldness against the devil!

Did you know that the devil cannot read your mind? He can only read your actions and your attitudes; he can only hear your confessions. So you need to be bold when you deal with him.

Some of us will wait a week before we resist him. We want to have a pity party first. We don't want to hear about God or about faith. We want someone to cook us a meal while we just lie in bed moping.

We want to hear sympathetic words such as: "You're such a great and wonderful man of faith. You deserve some pity. So you just stay there and rest awhile."

I know; I've done that. There have been times when I didn't want to say good confessions or fight the good fight of faith. I just wanted to feel sorry for myself.

But there comes a time when we have to be bold to fight the enemy. And there comes a time to be bold in witnessing, in telling people what we believe and what we stand for.

Let's look again at Acts 4:13 NKJV:

**Now when they saw the boldness of Peter and John, and perceived that they were uneducated and untrained men, they marveled. And they realized that they had been with Jesus.**

The important result of holy boldness is that other people will realize that you have been with God. It goes on in verses 29-31 NKJV to say this:

**"Now, Lord, look on their threats, and grant to Your servants that with all boldness they may speak Your word, by stretching out Your hand to heal, and that signs and wonders may be done through the name of Your holy Servant Jesus."**

**And when they had prayed, the place where they were assembled together was shaken; and they were all filled with the Holy Spirit, and they spoke the word of God with boldness.**

Notice that when the believers prayed, they were filled with the Holy Spirit; the result was that they spoke the Word of God with boldness.

Again, Proverbs 28:1 NKJV says:

**The wicked flee when no one pursues, But the righteous are bold as a lion.**

Then in Acts 9:27-29 NKJV the Bible says this about the apostle Paul:

**But Barnabas took him and brought him to the apostles. And he declared to them how he had seen the Lord on the road, and that He had spoken to him, and how he had preached boldly at Damascus in the name of Jesus.**

**So he was with them at Jerusalem, coming in and going out.**

**And he spoke boldly in the name of the Lord Jesus and disputed against the Hellenists, but they attempted to kill him.**

These verses show that sometimes people are not too happy when you get bold!

In First Thessalonians 2:2 NKJV Paul says:

**But even after we had suffered before and were spitefully treated at Philippi, as you know, we were bold in our God to speak to you the gospel of God in much conflict.**

When you speak the Word of God boldly, at times it will bring conflict. It will cause conviction in some people, but sometimes it will also create an uproar by upsetting other people.

I would rather have people walk out of the church service than fall asleep during it. I would rather have them hear the truth than listen to tradition and religion that offers nothing. I will preach the Word of God because the Word is the only thing that can truly change people's lives.

Now, listen to me: You can't compromise. Whenever you compromise in order to receive something you want, you will lose it anyway.

Take the example of a young woman who decides to go out with a man who isn't even saved. After a few months, he says, "Darling, if you really love me, you'll sleep with me." So she sleeps with him. But once he gets what he wants, he leaves her.

When you compromise, you lose both ways.

## How To Receive Boldness

We are to walk in a life of boldness. So how do we receive this boldness? Here are some ways:

**1. Ask for boldness in prayer.**

As we saw in Acts 4:29, the believers asked God to grant them the spirit of boldness that they might speak the Word of God. Verse 31 NKJV says:

**And when they had prayed, the place where they were assembled together was shaken; and they were all filled with the Holy Spirit, and they spoke the word of God with boldness.**

It's scriptural for you to say: "Lord, I don't want to be intimidated anymore by those people. I don't want to be fearful of the devil. I don't want to walk according to what people are going to think. So give me a spirit of boldness. I believe I receive it, in Jesus' name."

**2. Stay full of and controlled by the Holy Spirit.**

When you get full of the Holy Spirit, you will find yourself being much bolder than before. You will declare and do things you would not normally do if you were not full of the Holy Spirit.

Remember, once a person receives the Lord and is born again, he receives the Holy Spirit in a measure. Some great Christians have lived a life of integrity, but

171

have never been baptized in the Holy Spirit with the evidence of speaking in other tongues.

Galatians 5 talks about the fruit of the Spirit. When a person is born again, even if he doesn't believe in the baptism of the Holy Spirit with the evidence of speaking in other tongues, he has the potential to walk in all the fruit of the Spirit, such as love, joy, peace, self-control and patience.

There are some wonderful Christians who don't have the power in their lives to deal with demon activity. They don't have a prayer language that will move them into the realm of intercession. They don't operate in the gifts of the Holy Spirit that are mentioned in 1 Corinthians 12.

You see, Christians can receive revelation and excel in one area of their spiritual walk and not another. For example, did you know that seven years passed after Jesus' resurrection before the apostle Peter received the revelation that a Gentile could be saved?

Today you can hear about Christians who have been faithful, loyal, humble servants of Jesus and have walked for years in the Body of Christ with integrity, but who died sick. Why? Because they didn't have a revelation of God as *Jehovah Rapha*, **the Lord that healeth thee.** (Exodus 15:26.)

Just because someone excels in one area of his spiritual walk doesn't automatically mean he will excel in every other area.

Some Christians excel in the power of God. For example, the healing evangelists in the forties and fifties held meetings in tents, ministered to the sick, and operated in the gifts of the Holy Spirit. Several of these healing evangelists could tell people their names and where they were from, then by the Spirit they would say such things as, "You've had cancer for four years; be healed." And in Jesus' name, healing came!

172

But with some of those ministers, the fruit of the Spirit could not be found in their lives. Some of them cheated people; others went on the bottle.

You may say, "But how can someone who operates in the gifts of the Spirit so powerfully not have love, peace, and honesty? And how could God use anyone who drinks?"

Let me tell you something: If your life *inwardly* does not match the anointing and power of God *outwardly*, you will eventually destroy yourself.

Those men were greatly used of God, but some of them died young. One died an alcoholic. Although those ministers were not right inwardly, they could still get on a platform to preach, and God would bless and anoint them outwardly.

So I questioned God about it. I said, "God, I don't understand this. Why?"

That's when I found out this important truth about God: He is interested in helping as many people as possible when He exercises patience in His dealings with one person.

For example, a minister who isn't living the right life might preach to crowds of twenty thousand every night, and people might be getting saved and delivered. In that case, God may be as interested in helping those thousands as He is in exercising patience toward that minister for his sin.

Another important truth is that the gifts and the calling of God are without repentance. (Romans 11:29.) In other words, the gifts and callings God has given you will not always operate through you if you're not walking with God. But the minute you get back to a place in your spiritual walk where God can work through you, those gifts will begin to operate again. That means God never takes those gifts away; *we* separate *ourselves* from them.

Some of those preachers I mentioned just didn't walk in the wisdom of God. They never looked after their bodies or stayed physically fit. They didn't regularly wait before the Lord so that their relationship with Him could be strengthened. They just kept going and going and going, until eventually they got so far out that they couldn't come back.

For instance, if a preacher had a few drinks every night before stepping onto the platform, eventually he wouldn't know whose voice — God or the devil's — he was hearing.

So the gifts and callings are without repentance; but if our lives are not right before God, we can never operate accurately in those gifts.

If I spend time before the Lord in His Word and prayer, and I keep my life right before God, He will begin to speak and I will know His voice. I operate my ministry according to what I hear from Him that He wants to do through me.

In Acts 1:5,8 NKJV Jesus said:

**"For John truly baptized with water, but you shall be baptized with the Holy Spirit not many days from now...**

**"But you shall receive power when the Holy Spirit has come upon you; and you shall be witnesses to Me in Jerusalem, and in all Judea and Samaria, and to the end of the earth."**

In our lives we must seek both the *fruit* of the Spirit and the *power* of the Holy Spirit. Let's be people of integrity, honesty, kindness, gentleness, and self-control. But let's also be able to minister effectively, bringing deliverance to people by breaking the power of the devil over them. Remember, Jesus said, "God has anointed Me to preach the Gospel to the poor, to heal the brokenhearted, to set the captives free, to give sight to the blind, and to heal those who are oppressed." (Luke 4:18.)

Acts, chapter 2, tells us about the time the early church first received the Baptism of the Holy Spirit — the fullness of God's power.

**When the Day of Pentecost had fully come, they were all with one accord in one place. And suddenly there came a sound from heaven, as of a rushing mighty wind, and it filled the whole house where they were sitting. Then there appeared to them divided tongues, as of fire, and one sat upon each of them. And they were all filled with the Holy Spirit and began to speak with other tongues, as the Spirit gave them utterance.**

**Acts 2:1-4** NKJV

Then in Acts 2:16-20 NKJV Peter says:

**"But this is what was spoken by the prophet Joel:**
**'And it shall come to pass in the last days, says God,**
**That I will pour out of My Spirit on all flesh;**
**Your sons and your daughters shall prophesy,**
**Your young men shall see visions,**
**Your old men shall dream dreams.**
**And on My menservants and on My maidservants**
**I will pour out My Spirit in those days;**
**And they shall prophesy.**
**I will show wonders in heaven above**
**And signs in the earth beneath:**
**Blood and fire and vapor of smoke.**
**The sun shall be turned into darkness,**
**And the moon into blood,**
**Before the coming of the great and awesome day of the Lord.'"**

You may say, "That sounds terrible!" No, those are just manifestations of God; you just have to understand how God manifests Himself. He appeared to Moses in a burning bush. He came in a cloud on the Mount of Transfiguration. (Exodus 3:2; Matthew 17:1-5.)

Let me tell you something: What will be a terrible time for the world will be an exciting time for the Church! But God is not like some little weakling of a person who runs around, frantically trying to keep everything together. God is almighty; He is all-powerful. When He begins to manifest in His fullness, we will really see some signs and wonders, and the world will know something is coming that they have never known before.

**Then Peter said to them, "Repent, and let every one of you be baptized in the name of Jesus Christ for the remission of sins; and you shall receive the gift of the Holy Spirit."**

**Acts 2:38** NKJV

The wonderful thing about a gift is that you don't work for it; you just receive it. So you do the desiring for the fullness of the Holy Spirit; God will do the producing.

**"For the promise is to you and to your children, and to all who are afar off, as many as the Lord our God will call."**

**Acts 2:39** NKJV

The blueprint for the Church is to walk in the power of God through the Holy Spirit as is found in the Book of Acts. If you want to know how to run a church by the Holy Spirit, study the Book of Acts. It's amazing.

**Then the twelve summoned the multitude of the disciples and said, "It is not desirable that we should leave the word of God and serve tables.**

**"Therefore, brethren, seek out from among you seven men of good reputation [honesty], full of the Holy Spirit and wisdom, whom we may appoint over**

this business; but we will give ourselves continually to prayer and to the ministry of the word."

And the saying pleased the whole multitude. And they chose Stephen, a man full of faith and the Holy Spirit, and Philip, Prochorus, Nicanor, Timon, Parmenas, and Nicolas, a proselyte from Antioch, whom they set before the apostles; and when they had prayed, they laid hands on them.

Then the word of God spread, and the number of the disciples multiplied greatly in Jerusalem, and a great many of the priests were obedient to the faith.

And Stephen, full of faith and power, did great wonders and signs among the people.

Acts 6:2-8 NKJV

As we see in the Book of Acts, it is God's will for every layperson to have a ministry of reconciliation, a ministry of laying on of hands to the sick, a ministry that is full of faith and power. Such a ministry is not intended for just a select few.

### 3. Know the character of God.

Did you know that your faith begins where the will of God is known? I will be honest with you; when I went to Bible school, the two subjects that blessed me the most to learn and understand were *the character of God*, and *what God wanted to do in me and through me.* I found out that God wasn't out there all the time with a big stick, waiting for me to make a mistake so He could kill me.

There is a side of God that reveals His judgment and His righteousness, and that side is very real. But when you know the character of God in His fullness, you will come to know His love.

In order to live a godly, righteous, holy life, you have to be motivated by God's love, not by the idea that He is going to get you. If you have a "God-is-going-to-get-me"

177

attitude toward Him, you will never come into the intimate relationship with Him that you need.

But when you are motivated by the love of God, you will understand the judgment of God. You can't understand God and walk closely with Him until you get a revelation of the love He has for you.

I will prove this to you from the Word of God. Let's look first in Hebrews, chapter 4:

**And there is no creature hidden from His sight, but all things are naked and open to the eyes of Him to whom we must give account.**

**Seeing then that we have a great High Priest who has passed through the heavens, Jesus the Son of God, let us hold fast our confession. For we do not have a High Priest who cannot sympathize with our weaknesses, but was in all points tempted as we are, yet without sin. Let us therefore come boldly to the throne of grace, that we may obtain mercy and find grace to help in time of need.**

**Hebrews 4:13-16 NKJV**

Now let's look at Psalm 23. This is one of my favorite psalms. Did you know that David is not the subject of this psalm? The subject is the Shepherd. What God is trying to do here is to show you the character of the Shepherd. If you want to know what Jesus is like as the Shepherd, you will find it here. This describes Him totally.

**The Lord is my shepherd; I shall not want.**

**Psalm 23:1 NKJV**

I know the character of God, and I shall not want when He is my Source. I am as convinced as I could ever be that when I serve my Father God and live for Him, I become qualified for this blessing. When I walk with God to the best of my ability, I shall not want. I don't care what the economy or the circumstances of life may be. I don't care how bad things may look or how terrible things may seem. God is my Source!

**He makes me to lie down in green pastures; He leads me beside the still waters. He restores my soul....**

**Psalm 23:2,3** NKJV

If you have a problem in your mind, the Shepherd can restore it. I have seen God totally restore confirmed drug addicts in their mental realm.

**...He leads me in the paths of righteousness For His name's sake.**

**Yea, though I walk through the valley of the shadow of death, I will fear no evil; For You are with me; Your rod and Your staff, they comfort me.**

**You prepare a table before me in the presence of my enemies....**

**Psalm 23:3-5** NKJV

Now this can't be talking about heaven, because there are no enemies in heaven.

**...You anoint my head with oil; My cup runs over.**

**Psalm 23:5** NKJV

When you read that verse, you may wonder where people got all that nonsense that claims God isn't going to do anything and that He wants you to have nothing and to be nothing! Look at verse 6 NKJV:

**Surely goodness and mercy shall follow me All the days of my life; and I will dwell in the house of the Lord Forever.**

Just think about how good God is to give us a Shepherd Who loves us. I don't ever want out of God's kingdom, do you?

So apply these three principles to your life so you can walk in holy boldness: Ask God for boldness in prayer; stay full of and controlled by the Spirit; and become fully acquainted with the character of God. As you do,

# 8

## IMPACTING MEN HAVE SENSE ENOUGH NOT TO TOUCH THE BRIDE

### A CALL TO OBEDIENT PRAYER

*The bride of Christ today has been abused by people who have no right to touch her, because the Church has been reserved for Jesus alone. People have used the Bride to develop "empires," to get money, and to build their reputations.*

*One thing I know will be different about the <u>new thing</u> God is doing: It will be led by individuals who aren't taking the bride for their own selfish purposes, but are giving themselves to the bride because she belongs to Jesus.*

**— Sam Benson**

## 8

### *IMPACTING MEN HAVE SENSE ENOUGH NOT TO TOUCH THE BRIDE*

by Sam Benson

*Pastor, Destiny Christian Center*
*Puayallup, Washington*

Most of us know that the blood covenant is the basis for relationships in the Body of Christ, but we don't always understand completely what that means.

The Communion service is a memorial of the last Passover, when Jesus broke bread and drank wine with His disciples. The Passover itself was a memorial of the deliverance of the Israelites from Egyptian bondage through blood placed on the doorposts. And in turn, that event commemorated, or restated, the original blood covenant God had made with Abraham. That blood covenant — the Old Covenant — was fulfilled, or ratified, by Jesus on the Cross.

Many things are involved in making a blood covenant, and a thorough study of covenants is well worth the time involved. In order to understand what God is saying to church leaders today, we certainly should understand the following three things about a blood covenant relationship.

The first is this: *Everything I have is yours, if you ever need it.*

This principle should be the first thing understood when we make covenant with one another. And certainly it should be the first thing understood when we are born again, for at that time we enter into a blood covenant relationship with Jesus.

Covenant says there is nothing I can hold back from you if what I have can meet your need.

Another thing covenant means is this: *Everything that I am is yours, if you ever need me.* Not only what I *have,* but what I *am,* belongs to the one in covenant relationship with me.

When you view *covenant* that way, it helps gets rid of the shallowness in your relationships, doesn't it? When you understand the true meaning of *covenant,* you can eliminate just going through the motions in relationships and come to a place of real commitment to one another.

Jesus completely and totally gave of Himself. We rejoice in His love. We are strengthened in His love. We are encouraged by the commitment He made to us. We thank Him for it and certainly should not take it lightly. We need to always be aware that when He entered into covenant with mankind, it cost Him *everything.*

A third thing to remember is this: *Entering into covenant with Jesus places us into covenant with everyone else who has entered into covenant with Him.*

The Body of Christ is made up of brothers and sisters. We *are* the family of God. These are literal, not just spiritual, truths. But what does it mean to those of us who are set in positions of authority in the Body?

For an answer to this question, let's look at a statement Jesus made, found in the Book of Matthew. It is a statement that He said all men could not accept.

## A Eunuch Is in Charge of the Bride

**For there are eunuchs who were born that way from their mother's womb; and there are eunuchs who were made eunuchs by men; and there are also eunuchs who made themselves eunuchs for the sake of the kingdom of heaven. He who is able to accept this, let him accept it.**

**Matthew 19:12 NAS**

Many of us today don't understand what Jesus meant in this verse. We know what a eunuch is in the natural, but we don't understand what it is in the kingdom of God. A spiritual eunuch is *not* a guy with a high voice who has been emasculated. To understand this term, we need to look at what a eunuch did for a king in historical times in the Middle East.

A eunuch was in charge of the king's harem — all the king's wives. The eunuch was put in a position of looking after the king's bride (or brides). The king couldn't trust a natural, or normal, man not to succumb to the temptation of sampling the harem women. So certain men were emasculated and trained in the responsibilities of looking after the bride, or the brides, of the king.

The bride of Christ today has been abused by people who have no right to touch her, because the Church has been reserved for Jesus alone. People have used the bride to develop "empires," to get money, and to build their reputations.

One thing I know will be different about the *new thing* God is doing: It will be led by individuals who aren't taking the bride for their own selfish purposes, but are giving themselves to the bride because she belongs to Jesus.

Impacting men in this move of God will be those who have sense enough not to touch the bride. The bride has been raped, exploited, and plundered enough; she has been abused enough.

185

We are the ones called to help those who belong to Jesus. He's coming back for a glorious church without spot or wrinkle. (Ephesians 5:27.) Let's set ourselves to take care of the bride, to protect her, to see that she is cherished and made ready for the Bridegroom.

Let's make a commitment to the Church and say: "I'm not going to abuse you or use you to build my reputation or my treasury. Perhaps for the first time, I'm going to correctly discern the Body of Christ."

As impacting men (and women), let's take our place in this generation for the glory of God, and not for our own glory.

# IMPACTING MEN HAVE
# A CALL TO OBEDIENT PRAYER

_Prayer is war as it has never been waged in the natural realm._ Prayer is the pulling down of strongholds, because the "ozone layer," so to speak, in the Spirit realm is disintegrating, allowing attacks of the enemy to bombard the Body of Christ more than almost any time previously.

As the Church, we must go on the offensive today. We are going to win this war!

**— Kimble Knight**

## IMPACTING MEN HAVE A CALL TO OBEDIENT PRAYER

by Kimble Knight
*Rockwall, Texas*

I once received a little different insight on a passage in Judges 3. Usually, we hear this Scripture ministered in the positive sense of teaching us how to war against the enemy of our souls.

**Now these are the nations which the Lord left, to prove Israel by them, even as many of Israel as had not known all the wars of Canaan;**

**Only that the generations of the children of Israel might know, to teach them war, at the least such as before knew nothing thereof.**

**Judges 3:1,2**

God left the enemies in the land to teach the children of Israel how to war. However, I now see how this account also points to a different kind of warfare — one that has to do with prayer.

*Prayer is war as it has never been waged in the natural realm.* Prayer is the pulling down of strongholds, because the "ozone layer," so to speak, in the Spirit realm is disintegrating, allowing attacks of the enemy to bombard the Body of Christ more than almost any time previously.

Today many in the Body of Christ are experiencing a different dimension of warfare in their prayers. They have sensed their normal prayer times shifting to a

189

warfare-type of praying, as opposed to praying more general prayers.

I recently began to look at those verses in Judges and to think about the fact that God *left* the enemies in the land *to teach the Israelites war.* As I asked the Lord about that, I began to see two different kinds of warfare: war resulting from disobedience and war resulting from obedience.

God left the enemies in the land to test the Israelites — to *prove* them — because they had not done what Joshua had done. They hadn't followed the commandments of their fathers. Therefore, the warfare they were engaged in was a result of disobedience.

The difference between a war resulting from disobedience and one resulting from obedience is that the first type of war is *defensive,* and the second type is *offensive.*

When you and I as men or women of God have been disobedient in our walk, as Israel had been disobedient in Judges 2 and 3, it throws us into a defensive mode.

Have you ever seen someone who is very defensive? If you say the least little word to that person, he begins to justify, rationalize, and defend his stance. That person is in a "defensive war" mode. I think many in the Body of Christ are in that position today, particularly the younger men.

Many of us younger men have experienced times when our youthfulness has been despised. Therefore, we have too often gotten defensive, and we've poured the kerosene of our defensiveness on coals of zeal without using wisdom.

We get zealous and defensive, because we are maintaining a defensive war. It may look good, as if we are "doing a number" on the devil's head, all in the name of God. But it's a disobedient war we are engaged in. We are pushing back the darkness, but we aren't operating in obedience.

God left the enemies in the land *to teach His people obedience.*

If you are in right standing with God and are operating in His will, you can go forth in prayer and be mighty. You are to be on the offensive.

I believe God wants us to enter into an offensive war against our enemy, the devil. But first, we must be truthful with ourselves. Are we being obedient to what God has called us to do? Or are we in disobedience?

Second, we must find a place where we can be aggressive against the enemy, a place to go on the offensive. We must find that daily place of prayer.

I can't be on the offensive if I am not going forth to war daily. If I only respond to specific attacks that come at me, then I am just maintaining a defensive position.

If I am just "tooling along" in my ministry and waiting for an attack to come, I am not pressing forward against the gates of hell. That puts me on the defensive, on the run. That puts me in a position of justifying and rationalizing.

But if I am offensively attacking the enemy in the Spirit, then I am engaged in a war resulting from obedience. In that kind of war, I can always expect victory as the outcome!

Church, *we are on the offensive today.* We are going to win this war. So enter into the warfare. Don't wait for it to come to you. Put on the armor of God, and then go to war!

# 9

# THE INGREDIENTS FOR
# A FULFILLING MARRIAGE

*There are ingredients, thoughts, and attitudes that God put in the Word so that you could have a happy, fulfilled, and exciting marriage. But you have to follow the divine recipe.*

*If you will follow God's will, God's Word, and God's plan, you will have the good marriage He wants you to have.*

**— Casey Treat**

## THE INGREDIENTS FOR A FULFILLING MARRIAGE

by Casey Treat
*Pastor, Christian Faith Center*
*Seattle, Washington*

I want to bring to your attention the ingredients, thoughts, and attitudes that God gives us in His Word to help us have a happy, fulfilled, and exciting marriage.

Let's begin by looking at a passage from Ephesians 5:

**Wives, submit to your own husbands, as to the Lord. For the husband is head of the wife, as also Christ is head of the church; and He is the Savior of the body. Therefore, just as the church is subject to Christ, so let the wives be to their own husbands in everything.**

**Husbands, love your wives, just as Christ also loved the church and gave Himself for her, that He might sanctify and cleanse her with the washing of water by the word, that He might present her to Himself a glorious church, not having spot or wrinkle or any such thing, but that she should be holy and without blemish.**

**So husbands ought to love their own wives as their own bodies; he who loves his wife loves himself.**

**Ephesians 5:22-28 NKJV**

Now let's go to the Book of Proverbs, sometimes called the Book of Wisdom, for some other insights on the marriage relationship. In Proverbs 5, it says:

**Drink water from your own cistern, And running water from your own well.**

**Should your fountains be dispersed abroad, Streams of water in the streets?**

**Let them be only your own, And not for strangers with you.**

**Let your fountain be blessed, And rejoice with the wife of your youth.**

**As a loving deer and a graceful doe, Let her breasts satisfy you at all times; And always be enraptured [intoxicated] with her love.**

**For why should you, my son, be enraptured by an immoral woman, And be embraced in the arms of a seductress?**

**Proverbs 5:15-20 NKJV**

These Scriptures tell us that marriage doesn't have to be negative. It doesn't have to be painful and difficult. It doesn't have to be hard, and it doesn't have to end in divorce.

God is saying, "It isn't My will that you be alone." He has a higher life, a more fulfilling life, a more joyful experience for each of us to receive through the marriage relationship. If we will follow God's will, God's Word, and God's plan, we will have the good marriage He wants us to have. It's possible, and it's available to everyone.

There are a couple of quotes that I have adapted to marriage issues: one from Albert Einstein and another from Medical Doctor M. Scott Peck's book, *The Road Less Traveled*.[1]

Einstein applied his idea to science and to other facets of life, but I am applying it to marriage. Here's my adaptation of what Einstein said: The problems we face in marriage can't be overcome by the same thinking that got us into those problems.

## The Ingredients for a Fulfilling Marriage

In other words, because of pride, because of ego, because of false images that we have of ourselves, we often get into some painful situations in our marriage relationship. But too often we don't seek counsel or try to renew our minds with God's Word; we just keep thinking we can get ourselves out of our marital trouble.

If you have fallen in a hole in your marriage, you probably can't get yourself out; you need someone to throw you a lifeline. If your own thinking created the problem, then that same thinking isn't going to solve the problem. If you were so smart, you wouldn't have gotten yourself into that problem in the first place!

If your situation is ever going to change for the better, you have to be open to hear new thoughts, to receive new insights, to get godly counseling and teaching from someone qualified to help you, and then to make the necessary changes.

Once you receive new thoughts and learn new ways of doing things, then you can get yourself out of the problem in which you find yourself. The problems you are facing in marriage can't be changed by the same thinking that got you into them. It's "habit insanity" to think that you can keep doing the same wrong things over and over, and yet life will somehow get better.

It's foolish to think that when you continue to do what you have always done, the results will somehow suddenly start being different and the situation will just get better. It *won't* get better. *You* have to change.

You have to renew your mind by going to the Word to receive new thoughts, new insights, new perspectives. Then you will begin to see changes in your home.

In *The Road Less Traveled,* Peck says that life is hard; but when you recognize that fact and begin to take the necessary steps to make life good, life becomes easier. Adapting Peck's idea to marriage, I would say this: Marriage isn't easy, but realizing that fact will help you do the hard work of making your marriage the most rewarding and fulfilling part of your life.

No, marriage *isn't* easy. Just because you are a human being doesn't mean you will know how to be a good spouse. Just the fact that you're a man won't make you a good husband, nor will the fact that you're a woman make you a good wife.

The same is true about parenthood. Just because you're a male who can have children doesn't mean you would be a good father. And the fact that you're a female who can give birth to babies isn't a guarantee that you would make a good mother. You have to learn. You have to grow. You have to develop the skills that will make you a husband or wife, a father or mother.

When you recognize that developing a fulfilling marriage relationship isn't easy but that you *can* do it, you will be well on your way to a successful marriage.

That's why in our school, Christian Faith School, we want to teach our kids how to be married, how to be a husband or wife or a father or mother. I went to public school for twelve years, but not one time did my teachers ever teach me how to be a husband or father.

So we included that kind of training in our school program, believing that our children need to learn the skills necessary to have a successful family. If we take six months to teach them how to drive a car and years to teach them how to read and do their math, we need to take even *more* time to teach them how to be a husband or wife.

You see, so many of the skills that children need to learn are really quite simple. We should say to our sons, "Here's how to be a husband; here's how to treat your wife. It's plain and simple, black and white; it's right here in the Book."

## The Ingredients for a Fulfilling Marriage

But most young men haven't been taught how to be a good husband, so they act the way they saw their dad act, and they go through divorce the same way their dad did. All over the world today men and women experience these same pains and struggles in marriage, because they haven't been taught how to be a husband or wife.

### Follow the Recipe

If you don't put the right ingredients together when you are in the kitchen cooking or baking, then no matter how sincere, how passionate, or how committed you may be in your cooking efforts, your end result just won't taste good.

For example, I like hot cereal. But when I am cooking it, no matter how much I may desire a good-tasting bowl of cereal, I will end up with a bowl of bland cereal if I don't add the salt.

I can want my dinner to turn out well. I can want my cookies or my cake to come out of the oven tasting perfect. But if I don't mix in the right ingredients, no matter how passionately or how much I may want it, it just isn't going to happen. For instance, if I leave the flour out of the dough, I just won't end up with anything that looks or tastes like cookies!

Have you ever spent a long time cooking a dish that you were really excited about tasting? Your mouth watered as you waited for it to get done. Then you tried to hurry the process by putting it in the refrigerator to cool it off faster.

But when you sank your teeth into your masterpiece, you realized that you made a drastic mistake. Some ingredient was missing. You forgot something, whether it was the baking soda or the salt or the vanilla.

So, we have to get all the ingredients right in order to cook a dish successfully. We have to follow the recipe.

You see, so many Christian people love God with all their heart, give their tithes and offerings, and desire the blessings of God. But because they aren't putting the right ingredients into their home, nothing is working for them. Their cookies don't come out right, their cereal is really bland, and their marriage is a drag. Why? Because they have failed to use the right ingredients!

Success isn't about working *harder* as much as it is about working *smarter.* It isn't about just *wanting* a good marriage. Everyone *wants* their marriage to work. If success in marriage were based on *wanting* to make it work, everyone would have a good marriage. No one gets married with the desire to fail.

Many times people can even look as if everything is all right when things are definitely *not* all right at home. When they go to church, they smile as if they are happy. When they are with friends, they put on a front to give the impression that things are going well. But when these people "sink their teeth" into their marriage, it's obvious that some ingredients are missing.

So we have to put the right ingredients into our marriage relationship.

I believe that some people think if they just *want* their marriage to work, it will. Not so! They have to put in the right ingredients. Just the "want to" isn't enough.

Here are a few of the ingredients it takes to make a great marriage:

### Ingredient Number One: *Commitment*

Commitment is the top priority, the beginning, the foundation, and the starting point for a marriage.

If you can't make a commitment, then you aren't ready for marriage. If you are in a marriage but haven't made a total commitment, then your marriage can't be all God wants it to be until you do.

Your commitment is your agreement, your pledge, your vow to give yourself to your spouse for the rest of your years on earth. That's the only kind of commitment that will make a successful marriage.

Remember, the only illustration that God gives of the relationship between husband and wife is Christ and the Church. God is saying that Jesus' relationship to His Church is the only relationship that could possibly be compared to the marriage relationship.

Think about your relationship with Jesus. You can never really commit yourself to Him if you are holding back in any area, saying: "Jesus, You can be Lord of all except for my sex life; that's where I have my fun," or, "Jesus, You can be Lord of my life, except where money is concerned. I don't want You messing with that." You can't tell Him that you are going to keep certain parts of your life to yourself. If Jesus isn't Lord *of* all, He isn't Lord *at* all.

The same is true in marriage. You can't say to your spouse, "I give myself to you till death do us part — except for the little secrets I'm keeping to myself." You can't say, "I want my own time, and I want to do my own thing, because I deserve my privacy," or, "Remember our prenuptial agreement; I can still have what's mine."

That isn't commitment. That kind of attitude is according to the world, not the Word. There are no prenuptial agreements in the Bible. If you feel you need a prenuptial agreement, don't get married.

I really believe this is a word that young people need to hear. To a young person (in his or her late teens or early twenties) I would say, "You should make the decision and set your course to get married young." You may be told to wait until you are in your thirties, but I disagree. Here's why.

When two young people marry, they haven't had time to build a life on their own, so they don't really need a prenuptial agreement. They can commit themselves to one another and begin their lives together. They start with zero and work hard to help each other. They grow up together and build toward a life of prosperity.

In a healthy marriage, it isn't "my money" or "your money." You don't say, "You can't touch *my* things, and I won't touch *your* things because we made this agreement." You are to view your marriage relationship as *"our* life together."

I didn't have my own house to take care of before Wendy and I were married. I had always lived with my parents until she and I got "our house." I did go through a little stint with drug rehabilitation, but that was like being in my parents' house, because I was told how to do things.

The problem with so many people today is that, before getting married, they have already lived in their own house for five, ten, or fifteen years. They are thirty, thirty-five, or forty years old when they marry, so they already know how they like things kept around their house. Then a spouse comes into the picture with a different opinion as to where everything should go.

I think a spirit of fear and negativity comes on the scene when people wait and wait and wait to get married. They make it harder on themselves by waiting unnecessarily.

Now it's hard enough when you are brand new at living on your own. When you are young, you don't have a clue as to where and how things are done, so you and your spouse can learn about life together.

I say to a young person: "Find that young woman or that young man, join together, and grow up in the Lord. Then as you learn how to live life as an adult, you will build habits together."

## The Ingredients for a Fulfilling Marriage

If you talk to couples who have been married for forty or fifty years, you will find that they didn't have "his life" and "her life." The two of them have lived and worked and grown together.

A friend of mine was in ministry for more than twenty years before he got married. He had obtained everything on his own: his own house, his own ministry, his own staff, his own reputation. It was difficult for him when he brought a wife into the life he had already established. He constantly measured her by what he already had, and she had to fit into everything he was already doing.

When Wendy and I got married, I didn't have a schedule, a plan, or a life of my own, so she didn't have to fit into anything that I was already doing. We were able to build our lives together.

When a person's image, position, title, or assets are already established, it's difficult for that person to bring a spouse into the midst of it all. This is the kind of situation where prenuptial contracts and agreements are brought into the picture.

When older people enter into a marriage relationship, they have to make more changes than a young person. They have more habits to break and more sacrifices to make.

Let's say you are an older person whose spouse has died, and you want to be married again. You need to realize that it will be different this time than it was when you got married as a young person.

Thank God, you have maturity, understanding, and experience to draw from, but you also have developed some habits. You really want to keep doing things "the way you have always done them." But if you're going to make a total commitment to your new spouse, you will have to break some of those habits.

There can be no back doors. No ifs, ands or buts. No prenuptial agreements. It takes a hundred-percent commitment — *till death do us part.*

So the first ingredient to a great marriage is commitment. You have to commit yourself to that marriage relationship 100 percent, knowing that there is no way out.

The reason God set it up this way is that there will be days when the pressure is on and you will want to look for a way out. When life gets tough and all the fun seems to have faded away, you may think, *Gee, I must have missed it. Is there any way I can get out of this?*

But when there is no way out, you have to keep going forward. You have to figure out a way to make your marriage work. You *can* make it work if that's the way it has to be. But you will find another way out if you can.

When you got married, you made a commitment — an agreement, a pledge, a vow. Numbers 30:2 says:

**If a man vow a vow unto the Lord, or swear an oath to bind his soul with a bond; he shall not break his word, he shall do according to all that proceedeth out of his mouth.**

This verse is saying, "Men, if you have made a vow, you have to fulfill your word."

On the day Wendy and I got married, I said to her: "I give my life to you. I'll love you and honor you, support you and care for you till death do us part." As a Christian man, I must fulfill my word. If I will live by my vow, my marriage will work.

Then Numbers 30:3,4 says:

**If a woman also vow a vow unto the Lord, and bind herself by a bond...then all her vows shall stand, and every bond wherewith she hath bound her soul shall stand.**

This verse is saying, "Women, if you have taken a vow or given your word, then fulfill or follow through on that word."

Let's have some integrity and honesty in our lives. If we don't intend to follow through on our vow, then we shouldn't make it.

The wife may say, "But my husband didn't follow through on his vow." Oh, I see — because he's a liar, you can be a liar too!

Are we supposed to live like that? If so, then whenever there's a bad guy in town, I have the right to be a bad guy too. Are the actions and moral standards of other people to be the controlling factors of our decisions?

Again, the wife may say, "He isn't doing what he's supposed to do as a husband, so that gives me the right to divorce him." Oh, so now you don't have to do what you said that *you* would do? Is that the way it goes?

If we lived by that kind of mentality, we would all base our behavior on what other people do. Therefore, for instance, if you are a liar and a cheat, I can be one too. Is that how we are supposed to live? I think not.

So remember the first ingredient of a fulfilling marriage: *commitment.*

## Ingredient Number Two: *Sacrifice*

Sacrifice means giving up what is valuable or precious to you. It means giving up your treasure and giving up your rights.

Having worked with several Christians who went through a divorce, one of the most common questions I hear from them is this: "Don't I have the right to do what makes me happy?"

When they say that, I ask, "Well, can't you be happy in this marriage?"

"There's no way I could be happy," they say, and they start telling what their spouse has been doing.

Then I say, "But you said in your vow...."

They interrupt, "But don't I have the right to be happy? Don't I have the right to have some free time? Doesn't God want me to have a happy life?"

Here's the word of the Lord in response to such an attitude: "You gave up your rights when you made that marriage commitment."

It's just the same as when you had children: You gave up the right to sleep! Those kids didn't ask you to bring them into this world. But when you did, you gave up your right to privacy and to your own time.

Thank the Lord, there are ways that you and your spouse can work it out to spend some time away from the kids. You may have friends who take your children on an outing now and then so you and your spouse can spend a little time together — for an afternoon or even for an entire weekend.

But basically, when you married your spouse, you gave up your own rights. Then when you brought children into the world, you gave up some more rights. That's what being a husband or a wife, a father or a mother is all about. However, sacrifice doesn't always feel good.

In marriage, you can no longer have the attitude, "Well, I have the right to be happy!" You will be happy if you do what God has told you to do. But if you are seeking your own rights, you will be miserable. The Equal Rights Amendment doesn't work in the Bible, and it doesn't work in the home.

You see, so many of us think we are supposed to do what we feel like doing in our marriage. But we can't do that. We must sacrifice our feelings.

## The Ingredients for a Fulfilling Marriage

God said in Romans 12:1 that as Christians, we are to present our bodies a living sacrifice. So when we come to the altar of marriage, we lay ourselves down on that altar. We say: "I give myself as a sacrifice on the altar of marriage. I sacrifice my life; I give up *my* rights, *my* time, *my* money, *my* house. Now it's all ours."

There is one problem, however, about being a *living* sacrifice: When the heat gets turned on and when the fire starts building in our lives, we living sacrifices start feeling the pressure! Then when things get really hard, we come crawling down off the altar. Right? That's when we have to say to our flesh, "Get back up on that altar!"

Now understand what I am saying about sacrifice. As individuals, we do have free time and our own rights. But we aren't fighting for our rights as individuals; we're fighting for our marriage and for our children. We aren't fighting for what "I want," but for what *God* wants and for what our family needs.

In America, we have a selfish mentality. We say, "But don't I have the right to feel good?" Yes. After we have sacrificed ourselves, we will feel good, knowing we have done the right thing and have honored God. And God will bless us for it. There will be fulfillment and happiness and joy. But those blessings won't come by you doing your own thing and sacrificing your family; they will come as you sacrifice yourself *for* your family.

I don't know how many people have had the attitude, "Don't I have the right to feel good?" but then have come to me later and said, "Casey, I still don't feel good. I left the husband who was making me miserable. Why am I'm still miserable? And I don't have those kids around me anymore who were messing up my schedule. How come I'm not happy?"

You see, you don't get joy by fighting for your rights; you get joy by making the sacrifice to follow the plan of God.

### Ingredient Number Three: *Understanding*

Webster's Dictionary says *understanding* means to comprehend or to be sympathetic and tolerant of another's thoughts, feelings, or behavior. When we think of understanding, we immediately think of our desire for other people to understand *us*.

When my wife and I get into an argument, this is my attitude: "Now, Honey, if you'll really listen and understand what I'm saying, you'll recognize that I'm right, because I know what it's all about."

Of course, she feels the same way and says, "If you'll just listen to me and understand me, you'll find out *I'm* right."

We need to take on this perspective: *I want to understand others before I even consider being understood.*

What are we doing when we take this position? We are giving out understanding.

What happens when we give out understanding? We receive understanding in return.

You see, the principle of giving and receiving works in every part of life.

If I seek to understand, I will receive the blessing of being understood. But if I always try to get others to understand me, then I will never receive. I will shut off the flow that leads to understanding.

When any group — whether a race, a nation, or a gender of people — starts fighting intensely to get the world to listen and to understand, then everybody backs off and closes their ears. No one wants to hear. But when people rise above their own selfish interests to try to understand others, then they will eventually reap the joy of being understood.

Now here's a question for you husbands: Do you understand your wife's menstrual period? I certainly don't understand that area of my wife's life. It's a tough time of the month that creates a "funky" attitude in some women. They often experience feelings of pain and problems in their bodies because of changes in their hormones.

I don't understand it, so what do I do? As the man of God who thinks he knows all the answers, I try to get my way. I want Wendy to overcome problems with her menstrual period, so I say: "Come on, Honey — keep a stiff upper lip! You're a faith woman who is redeemed from the curse. I'll tell you what to do to overcome a menstrual period: just speak the Word over that thing in Jesus' name."

Let me tell you from my own experience: That's a stupid way to act toward your wife!

So what am I to do if I want to have all the ingredients to a great marriage? I don't just want Wendy to understand *me*; I want to understand *her*. So I say: "Tell me about the physical part, about the pain you feel. Tell me about the emotional part, about the thoughts and feelings that you're having. I want to understand what's going on inside you."

It seems that we husbands have been so slow to understand our wives. Many of us have never really sought to understand what their bodies go through during their menstrual cycle. We have just wanted them to get tough and deal with their emotions.

Come on, husbands, let's wise up and be willing to learn and to understand our wives!

On the other hand, our wives need to understand when we husbands miss it and ask them, "What's the problem? Why are you acting this way?" Wives have to see that we husbands just don't get it. I mean, we don't have hormonal changes; we don't go through all those feelings every month the way our wives do. So instead of our wives getting mad at us for being unaware of what they're going through, they must try to understand *our* perspective.

If both husband and wife are seeking to understand, they both will be understood. They will be giving *and* receiving, sowing *and* reaping understanding.

### Ingredient Number Four: *Trust*

Webster's says *trust* means to put confidence in, to believe in, to have settled assurance about your spouse's words and actions. Of course, along with trust comes trustworthiness.

If you were to say to me, "I just saw your wife buying whiskey at the liquor store. I know it was Wendy. I recognized her car. I saw her clothes and her hair. It was Wendy."

Without thinking, I would say, "No, I'm sure it wasn't Wendy."

I don't have to ask. I don't have to check. I don't have to wonder. I don't even have to think about it. I just know it wasn't my wife. You see, I know her, and I trust her.

Now, many of us grew up in a relatively untrusting environment, so we don't understand trust. You see, when trust is violated, the human response is to distrust the person who violated that trust. And if we listen to our human reasoning, we think that it's okay to respond that way.

We say, "I can't trust you now because you lied to me." But that isn't the biblical perspective. The biblical perspective is to give, even when someone doesn't give back to you; to trust, even when your trust is abused.

When our spouse violates our trust, we need to respond the same way a good parent responds to his or her children when they don't do what they say they will do. For example, think about what happens when parents tell their kids to clean their room, and the kids just go to their room and play for twenty minutes.

As a father, I know that scenario well. I have a child who, in the time it takes him to turn around, can forget what I told him to do. He can even be on his way to obey me and still end up doing something totally different.

When that happens, I say to my son, "Didn't Daddy tell you to do this?" Then he gets a look on his face that says he has some faint memory of it.

So again I say to him, "Go clean your room."

"Okay," he says, and away he goes.

When he comes back later, I say, "Did you clean your room?"

"Yep."

Being an experienced and wise father, I say: "Now, Dad is going to check your room in fifteen minutes. I want to see the bed made, the clothes picked up, the T-shirts folded, and the tennis shoes put away. Okay?"

When those fifteen minutes have passed, I go upstairs to his room and find that the bed is still a mess. His shoes and clothing are scattered everywhere.

Now if we were going to act like the world, what would we do? We would grab our child and say, "I told you to clean your room! Don't lie to me anymore! See, you did-n't clean your room!"

After that happened a couple of times, we would say to our children, "Go clean your room. I'll be coming back in fifteen minutes to see if you did it." A few minutes later, we would ask them again, "Did you clean your room?" If they said, "Yeah," we would say, "No, you didn't!"

Sometimes it seems that every time I go and check on my son's progress in cleaning his room, I find tennis shoes on the floor and clothes on the bed. Over and over again I go get him and say, "Come on, I'll show you. See, I said you didn't clean your room!"

Often we parents feel justified in not trusting our kids because every time we check, we find they didn't do what they said they would do. But what are our kids supposed to do? Their brains are still developing; they are in a process of figuring out the world. Therefore, our mistrust is not justified.

As parents, we have to trust our children again and again. We have to say over and over, "Okay, in fifteen minutes, I'll be back to check." And when we go back to check on their work once again, we don't give up if they haven't done it. We say, "Come on, Son. Daddy told you to get this done. Come on."

You have to keep trusting that child to do what he has been told to do. And as you sow *trust* in him, you build *trustworthiness* in him.

Now, the same kind of situation can occur between husbands and wives.

For example, the husband says, "I'll be home at five o'clock." Then at five-thirty, he comes walking in the door. He does that for a few weeks, a few months, a few years. After a while, the wife doesn't believe a word he says. When he tells her, "I'll be home at five," she thinks, *Well, maybe he'll be here by six.* She knows he's lying about it.

He starts making excuses and rationalizing why he's always late, saying, "Oh, things got in the way. The boss came in. The phone rang." At times he might be late for legitimate reasons; however, most of the time he's just lying. But he won't just admit to his wife, "I lied."

Years go by, and he never shows up on time. His wife doesn't trust his word anymore, so she always plans on dinner being late. He walks in knowing that she doesn't trust him. It's in his mind that if he showed up on time, she would be shocked.

So this husband's word isn't any good. He knows it and she knows it, and the whole family relationship has been built on a lack of trust.

Now what would happen if the wife still trusted her husband every time he told her he was going to do something, even though she knew he hadn't been keeping his word?

What if at five o'clock, dinner is on the table, and the kids are sitting down ready to eat? The husband doesn't show up until five-forty-five. The dinner is cold. The kids are nervous.

He says, "Well, Honey, you know I'm usually late."

She replies, "But you said five o'clock, so we were ready at five because I trust you."

Trust breeds trustworthiness. After that happens a few times, he may say, "Guys, I told my wife I would be home at five o'clock, and she's counting on me because she trusts me. I have to be there."

You see, when we distrust our spouse, we are just adding to the problem. We have to keep trusting, even when that trust is violated. We may get hurt, but we have already sacrificed our rights on the altar of marriage.

So we have to build on trust and trustworthiness in our marriage by giving out trust to our spouse, whether it is deserved or not. If we would walk in "honest submission" and deal in truth, not lies, we would stop faking with each other, and we would start having better relationships.

"Yeah, but he lied to me! He went out with another woman! He committed adultery! How can I trust him now?"

It's a choice. If you are at the point where you can't trust your spouse, then you never will have a great marriage. It's as simple as that.

The husband may not deserve his wife's trust. When he walks through the door, what he really deserves is for his wife to hit him in the jaw! *Pow!* The wife says, "That's what you deserve for that fornication you committed six years ago!" *Pow!* "And that's for the adultery you committed ten years ago!" That husband may deserve to get punched in the nose every day for the rest of his life. But that does *not* make for a good marriage!

How many times does she have to hit him before she just chooses to trust again? How long does she and her husband have to fight over that old hurt? How often should that failure be brought back up again?

The failure that caused the hurt and the pain could have been adultery, or it could have been a business failure, such as having to file for bankruptcy. But no matter what that failure was, how many times is the spouse who failed going to be reminded of it before the other spouse chooses to trust again?

Without trust, you can't have a great marriage. And *giving trust* breeds *trustworthiness*.

### Ingredient Number Five: *Communication*

Real communication occurs when both parties share their thoughts and feelings in a way that each can understand the other's position. Both husband and wife have to talk.

It's so silly when we communicate by sign language and grunts or when we express our thoughts by slamming the door and stomping down the hallway.

For example, the husband may say, "Well, you know how I feel about that." Then he expects the wife to figure out what he's talking about.

That isn't good communication. We don't live in the Stone Age. We don't share by grunting, by smacking rocks, or by dragging people around by their hair. We share by our language, by our words. We communicate by talking with one another.

There are some husbands in the church who are doing a certain thing in the marital sexual relationship that their wives hate. But the wife hasn't told her husband, because she won't communicate. So when he does it, he thinks he's being cool. He thinks she likes it, and she may have been hating it for years.

But the wife won't talk about the problem. She's afraid that if she says anything now, she will be embarrassed because she has let it go on for so long. That's why it's so important to communicate.

You have no right to be mad and upset with your spouse about what you don't like, but you allow it because you won't communicate. "But he should know better." No, he shouldn't. "But she should know that." No, she shouldn't.

We may say to our spouse, "But don't you know how I feel?" Maybe he (or she) does. But if we don't communicate our feelings clearly in words that can be understood, then we can't hold our spouse responsible for knowing how we feel. And *yet* we seem to make that mistake so often in our marriages!

Now, I talk a lot. Talking is my life. But when it comes to my relationship at home between me and my wife, I have to *make* myself express my thoughts. I often get to a point in a conversation where I just want to say to Wendy, "Oh, you know what I'm thinking." But she doesn't!

Many people make a big deal about body language. But at best, body language is limited communication. Too often it can be misread.

One spouse may say, "I thought you were mad about that." The other spouse replies, "No, I was mad about something else."

You can't decipher through body language what's going on in your spouse.

So the husband and wife have to talk; they have to communicate. They should be talking about all kinds of subjects, including their sexual relationship, their finances, and the scheduling of their time.

Whatever you hide and cover will become like a cancer that destroys your marriage. What you talk about will be open to the light, and the light of God's Word will keep it clean and pure. Always remember this:

Hide and Cover = Cancer

Openly Talk About = Light and Blessing

Whatever you allow in your life that makes you hide and sneak around and lie to your spouse becomes like a cancer in your marriage. But what you talk about openly will stay pure in the light of God's Word.

### Ingredient Number Six: *Love*

Love is caring. Love is giving without selfishness and without conditions.

There are several Scriptures on love. Let's look at some of them.

**...the love of God is shed abroad in our hearts by the Holy Ghost which is given unto us.**

**Romans 5:5**

**...faith which worketh by love.**

**Galatians 5:6**

Maybe you have been trying to get God to answer your prayers, but nothing is happening. You think, *Why is my faith not working?* The answer may lie in the fact that faith works by love. If you will start loving your spouse, God will start hearing your prayers.

**And walk in love, as Christ also hath loved us, and hath given himself for us an offering and a sacrifice to God for a sweetsmelling savour.**

Ephesians 5:2

**Husbands, love your wives, and be not bitter against them.**

Colossians 3:19

To the elder women, the Bible says:

**...teach the young women to be sober, to love their husbands, to love their children.**

Titus 2:4

**Beloved, let us love another: for love is of God; and every one that loveth is born of God, and knoweth God.**

**He that loveth not knoweth not God; for God is love.**

1 John 4:7,8

If you don't love your spouse, are you really a Christian? Scripture says that if you don't love, you don't know God. You may say, "But I confessed Him as my Savior." Well, the fruit of your confession is love toward people.

**Hatred stirreth up strifes: but love covereth all sins.**

Proverbs 10:12

**And above all things have fervent love for one another, for "love will cover a multitude of sins."**

1 Peter 4:8 NKJV

What does it mean, "Love covers a multitude of sins"? It *doesn't* mean we are to excuse and to rationalize another person's weaknesses; rather, it means we are to cover and to protect the person who has the weaknesses.

In 1 Peter 4:8, when it refers to *sin*, it is really talking about the times we miss it — those times when we aren't the person we should be. It's talking about the times the woman isn't the wife she needs to be, but rather points out the faults of her husband; or the times when the husband points his finger at his wife and says accusingly, "You need to be a submissive Christian wife the way the Bible says."

Love covers, protects, guards, and shields when others miss it. You know, if you only focus on what is wrong, you will find something wrong everywhere. But love covers a multitude of sins. So rather than squabbling over what you don't like about your spouse, just let love cover it.

I have talked with people who have been married for thirty, forty, and fifty years. They don't even know what they don't like about their spouse. They have been working together and loving each other for so long that all those things they didn't like have just disappeared.

But if you focus on a problem and pick on it, it will only get worse.

Remember how we were as kids? Once we got a little hole in our pocket, before long we could put our entire hand through that opening. In the same way, when we are immature, we pick on the faults of another and focus on the negative. And we end up just making matters worse.

We often do the same thing in our marriage relationship. We get so stuck on what we don't like about our spouse that we forget all the good qualities that caused us to want to be with her (or him) in the first place.

But love covers a multitude of failures and weaknesses — and that's the main ingredient that has to be in *every* marriage!

# 10

# *THE ABILITY TO LEARN FROM THE PAST*

*There has been a major move of God in this century about every forty years and a minor one about every twenty years.*

*We are nearing the end of this century, and it would seem that we are overdue for a major forty-year move of the Spirit — if we are seeing God's timetable clearly. (God certainly won't be locked into our timetable!) I do foresee such a move, however, and it will be led by impacting men and women like those of the past who won't be intimidated by either the world or the devil. They will be pure, full of integrity, and full of God.*

*However, I believe we must not only be inspired by the exploits of past spiritual leaders, but we must also learn from their mistakes. Many of the great men and women of God in the early days of this century fell into varying degrees of sin. Some saw a slow disintegration of their ministries because they knew <u>the acts of God</u> without knowing <u>the ways of God</u>. Others died early deaths.*

*God's next move will come completely into being when impacting men and women lay hold of the kingdom purely and in line with God's ways.*

**— Ron McIntosh**

# 10

## THE ABILITY TO LEARN FROM THE PAST

by Ron McIntosh

*President, Ron McIntosh Ministries*
*Tulsa, Oklahoma*

I have heard that the last prophecy of the late Smith Wigglesworth, one of the great spiritual figures in the early days of the twentieth century, was this:

"The last great wave of the Spirit will be led by young men and women of force."

When I asked God what it means to be a *forceful man,* an experience that my wife Judy and I had in East Texas came to mind. We had just been through a strenuous stretch of ministry, so we decided to take a mini-vacation to visit some friends in Dallas. Our friends took us out to eat at a restaurant where the waiters and waitresses all dress as fictional characters.

Mixed in with Batman, Wonder Woman, Indiana Jones, and Bugs Bunny was the devil! And he was *our* waiter!

My friend said, "Ron, if I had known the devil was going to wait on our table, I never would have brought you here."

I calmly reassured him, saying, "That's okay, Bill. I have been looking for a face-to-face encounter with the devil all day long."

The waiter, garbed in red suit, horns, pitchfork, tail, and the whole works, sauntered up to our table and in his vilest-sounding voice said, "Hi! I'm the devil."

To that, I quickly replied, "Hi! I rebuke you in Jesus' name!"

"You what...?" he said. Then he sheepishly went to get menus, keeping a wary eye on me.

When he said, "Follow me to the salad bar," I replied, "No. *You* follow *me.* I don't follow the devil anywhere." After a good laugh, I had the opportunity to witness to the young man throughout our meal.

God told me later that that was exactly how He wanted me to treat the devil in real life. "I want you to be forceful in the spiritual realm," the Lord said. And the forceful, make an impact.

In many of the places I travel and minister, people are confused, discouraged, disillusioned, and intimidated by what has been going on in the church for the past several years. Many are unsure about what to do and afraid to believe God in this hour.

If we are to be forceful men and women, we must not be fearful at the "shaking" of God or intimidated by the schemes of the devil. We must be like **...the children of Issachar, which were men that had understanding of the times, to know what Israel [God's people] ought to do...** (1 Chronicles 12:32).

I believe in my spirit that God is about to send a great wave of revival across the earth. Satan would like to confuse and intimidate us; instead, we must understand the hour and respond forcefully to God's voice.

One of my passions has been to study past Pentecostal, neo-Pentecostal, and Charismatic revivals. I've had two reasons for my interest:

1. To learn what promoted the waves of God.
2. To learn what hurt or stopped the moves of God.

I believe one of the mandates of my life is to warn people not to make the same mistakes that previous generations of Christians made.

One of the most interesting facts I have learned in my studies is that the past moves of God were *launched and stopped by similar things.*

Truly, I believe God is raising up a new generation of pure, Holy Spirit-filled, unintimidated, committed, and holy young men and women who won't make the mistakes of the past and will launch and perpetuate the greatest move of God's Spirit since Pentecost. To help us understand how to prepare for this, I want to first look back at some past exploits of spiritual leaders, and then look forward at ways we can learn from them.

## A Look Back

There has been a major move of God about every forty years in this century and a minor one about every twenty years. Let's start with a look at John Alexander Dowie, who ministered just before the turn of the century in Australia — even before the Azusa Street outpouring of modern Pentecostalism.[2]

Dowie received a revelation of healing from Acts 10:38 during a time of plagues that beset his continent. After receiving the revelation of God's healing power, he saw a young girl healed. From that point on, no one else in his church died from the plague, while the people of the city kept dropping like flies all around them.

Dowie later moved to America, settling near Chicago. Through Dowie's ministry in that area, a tremendous move of healings and miracles took place. Meanwhile, the secular press fought him, and during one particular year he was arrested on dozens of occasions for "practicing medicine without a license."

Finally, he moved northward in Illinois and established his own town, called Zion City. Within two years, ten thousand people lived in Zion City, constituting both the town's population and Dowie's congregation.

Dowie had little regard for doctors, and the entire city believed that the healing power of God would sustain them. Whether you personally believe that or not, the result for Zion City was a tremendously high health rate compared to the population at large. Dowie brought a "healing consciousness" to America.

During that same period of time, a woman named Maria Woodworth-Etter began a miracle ministry under much stress and persecution. The persecution she endured resulted first from the fact that she was a woman preacher, and second, from the healings and miracles that followed her ministry.[3]

Reports from that time claim that the anointing in her meetings was so strong, people fell into trances or were slain in the Spirit miles away from where her meetings were located. I think you can agree that such occurrences were a real manifestation of God's power.

Then in 1900, a man named Charles Parham began a Bible school in Topeka, Kansas, where students hungering for the presence of God were drawn by the possibility that the baptism of the Holy Spirit might be valid for their day.[4]

In a watch-night service, some of Parham's students began actively seeking this experience. At about midnight as the twentieth century dawned, eighteen-year-old Agnes Osnes asked Brother Parham to lay hands on her to receive the baptism. As soon as he did, she was filled with the Holy Spirit and began speaking in other tongues.

A mini-revival broke out, and it is said that this young lady could speak no English for three days. A few days later, Parham and other students also received this experience — a precursor of the Pentecostal Movement.

The citizens of Topeka asked Parham and his students to leave, so Parham relocated the Bible school to Houston, Texas. It was there that a one-eyed black man from Los Angeles named William Seymour heard of this experience. Overwhelmed with the revelation, he returned home to seek God about it.

In 1906, in an abandoned church on a street named Azusa in Los Angeles, California, the Spirit of God fell on Seymour and a small group of believers. For more than three years, day and night, God's miracles occurred in their midst. People were filled with the Spirit, every imaginable need was met, and God's healing virtue was powerfully manifested.

On one particular night, the building appeared to be on fire from the outside — so much so that the fire department came to put out the fire! The building was on fire with the fire of God, but like Moses' bush, it was not consumed.

People two or three blocks away from the Azusa Street revival would be slain in the Spirit. The presence of the Lord lifted after three and a half years, but not before virtually every nation in the world was touched by the Azusa Street Pentecostal revival, the product of the obedience of one humble man — William Seymour.

About twenty years later, God established another group of revivalists, including such spiritual leaders as John G. Lake, Aimee Semple McPherson, and Smith Wigglesworth. Some of these great men and women of God were from America, and some were from Great Britain.

There were reports that Hollywood designers would visit Sister McPherson's Angelus Temple to get ideas from her fabulous sets and costumes that accompanied her illustrated drama-sermons.[5] The world was looking to the church for ideas! This is again to be a pattern in the last days. (Micah 4:1,2.)

In Africa, John G. Lake established one of the most miraculous post-Pentecostal ministries to date. Later he settled in Spokane, Washington.

Lake's ministry produced approximately 100,000 documented healings in five years![6] Government agencies investigated his ministry, and unlike Dowie's experience, it was openly acknowledged that Spokane was the healthiest city in this country because of Lake's ministry.

Perhaps the most miraculous ministry of that era was that of Smith Wigglesworth. A minimum of fourteen people were raised from the dead under Wigglesworth's ministry. Many other astounding miracles took place, such as people's limbs being restored.

Then as suddenly as it began, the revival era ended. By the early Thirties, after the decline of Billy Sunday's ministry, it was over. But in 1947, a new era began. A healing revival started that shook the world. William Branham, a humble Baptist minister, came on the scene operating in the Holy Spirit's gift of word of knowledge.[7]

I like to call Branham the *initiator* of the "Voice of Healing Revival," but I believe that Oral Roberts was the main *innovator* of that period. Roberts was the first to display God's healing power before the nation on television. Perhaps more than any other man, he can be credited with awakening the modern church to God's healing and miracle power.

Then other great ministries came on the scene, such as the ministries of Jack Coe, A. A. Allen, T. L. and Daisy Osborn, W. V. Grant, Raymond T. Richey, and Kenneth E. Hagin. These men and women brought healing "out of the backwoods" and into the consciousness of the world.

In 1958, almost as suddenly as it began, the "Voice of Healing Revival" apparently ended. Then in 1967, the

"Jesus Movement" swept the country and "Word" teaching surfaced. Also, in the '60s and '70s, the world was awakened to the baptism of the Holy Spirit and the miracle-working nature of God through the Charismatic Renewal.

Now we are nearing the end of the century, and it seems we are overdue for a major forty-year move of the Spirit — if we are seeing God's timetable clearly. (God certainly will not be locked in to *our* timetable!) I do foresee such a move, however, and it will be led by forceful men and women like those of the past who won't be intimidated by either the world or the devil. They will be pure, full of integrity, and full of God.

However, I believe we must not only be inspired by the exploits of past spiritual leaders, but we must also learn from their mistakes. Many of the great men and women of God in the early days of this century fell into varying degrees of sin. Some saw a slow disintegration of their ministries because they knew the *acts of God* without knowing the *ways of God.* Others died early deaths.

## Periods of Transition

Between the closing of one move of God and the beginning of the next one, there is what I call a "period of transition." During this time, a "changing of the guard" occurs, as new leadership emerges on the scene. Often, the church and the general public will focus in on the shortcomings of ministries; therefore, these transition periods can be times of confusion, with people wondering what is really going on.

When Judy and I were about to have our first baby, we took Lamaze courses to help with her delivery. We learned all the breathing techniques for difficult times during labor. As we practiced, I would say, "Breathe, Darling," and she would breathe in and out, saying, "Hee,

hee, ho," according to the techniques she had learned. Everything seemed wonderful.

Finally, the fateful day arrived, and we went to the hospital. I did everything I was supposed to do. I wiped her brow and fed her ice chips. Every time she had a little pain, I would say, "Breathe, Darling," and she would dutifully breathe in and out, saying, "Hee, hee, ho."

Everything was going wonderful — until we hit *transition*. Only a woman who has had a baby can comprehend the difference in pain that comes at this time.

I would say, "Breathe, Darling," and she would say through gritted teeth, *"You* breathe!"

Proper breathing techniques went out the window. Why? The pain in "transition" had changed her perspective. No longer was she totally aware of everything around her.

It's the same way with transition in the Spirit. People are confused, not totally cognizant of everything around them, and their perspectives change.

I once heard the late Rev. Bob DeWeese (formerly an associate evangelist in the Oral Roberts Ministry) say, "The people who most longed for a move of the Spirit in 1947 were among those who rejected it when it came."

Why is this true? The key is that during the transition time between moves of God, people either become disillusioned and back off from spiritual things, *or they press into God.* Those who back off may miss the new move because it doesn't look like the old one. Those who look for God to do things the same way in each move will miss it.

However, those who press into God are alert in their spirits. They receive revelation, as Anna and Simeon did when Jesus was born. (Luke 2:22-38.)

Revelation always goes against traditional thinking. Those who receive revelation in their spirits slowly begin to pick up momentum; then they move into the next work of God.

It is during this time that new leadership emerges. People begin to question their spiritual roots, and those with spiritual "ears" begin to move forward to the challenge of the hour. Usually, the move forward is accompanied by great skepticism from those who don't see or understand what is happening.

## A Look Forward

We must learn from our predecessors so that we won't be prone to make the same mistakes today.

When the Voice of Healing Revival came to an end about 1958, G. H. Montgomery studied the causes that stopped the move. In 1962, he wrote a series of articles for *International Healing Magazine* entitled "The Enemies of the Cross."[8] Montgomery summarized what he thought were the causes of God's moves being stopped — factors that could be categorized as abuses. I have summarized his findings:

1. Many of the evangelists were *too independent* in their ministries.

Each ministry operated autonomously, leaving ministers to fall prey to their own frailties because they didn't have any oversight. In other words, they were submitted to no other authority and certainly not to one another. (Ephesians 5:21.)

2. Some of the evangelists fell into the trap of *materialism*, instead of true prosperity.

There *is* a difference between Biblical prosperity and the quest for materialism. God's perspective on wealth is to see His kingdom established on earth. (Deuteronomy 8:18.) Montgomery believed that many evangelists of the past moves had become ensnared in their quest for personal gain.

3. There were reports that some of these evangelists had problems with *drinking*, which probably was a reaction to the stress of ministry.

4. Some of the evangelists had problems with other fleshly sins such as *drugs*, *wife abuse*, and *prostitution*.

5. Montgomery charged that some evangelists were guilty of *exaggerated claims of results*.

For example, he cited claims of Jamaican converts by various evangelists — claims that, when added up, totaled three million converts in Jamaica in one year. The problem was, there were only 1.6 million people on the island at the time!

We must understand that the Spirit of Truth can only anoint us in proportion to our truthfulness.

6. Montgomery also claimed that many ministries of that time began to use *fraud*, *gimmickry*, and *manipulation* to keep themselves solvent.

The Holy Spirit has no other choice than to expose such actions. We find the precedent for this in Acts 5 where Ananias and Sapphira were dealt with. Thank God, the Holy Spirit has been long-suffering with the present-day church so far!

7. There was *widespread diversion of funds* to purposes other than those for which they were solicited.

When I first read these seven charges, I thought they could have been written much more recently than in 1962. Many of the ministries of that time were undoubtedly innocent of these charges. Unfortunately, the innocent ministries were often lumped in with the guilty ones.

When these kind of abuses become prevalent in a move of God, then God has no alternative: He must bring the move to an end if His people stray from His ways. Otherwise, it would ultimately discredit His name.

People wouldn't be able to see any difference between the actions of His people and those of a corrupt world.

We must remember that the *acts* of God won't go very far without the *ways* of God. One presupposes the other. Psalm 103:7 says:

**He made known his *ways* unto Moses, his acts unto the children of Israel.**

In Exodus 33:13-15 NIV Moses cried out to the Lord:

**"If you are pleased with me, teach me your ways so I may know you and continue to find favor with you."**

The Lord replied (v. 14):

**"My Presence will go with you, and I will give you rest"** [fulfillment of the promise].

Then Moses said (v. 15):

**"If your Presence does not go with us, do not send us up from here."**

Why was it so important to Moses to know the ways of God? Moses knew that the continued presence of the Lord was found in following His ways. Without God's ways, His acts would have to cease.

*That is precisely what has happened to every move of the Holy Spirit.* As people forgot the ways of God, His acts slowly came to an end. "Transitions" then followed until the next generation learned to again follow God's ways.

Reading Montgomery's conclusions prompted me to ask the question: "What are the keys that promoted revival, and what factors brought the revivals to an end?" Here are what I consider to be ten such keys:

1. *Christians need fraternal fellowship.*

No longer can Christians afford a lack of accountability or a lack of fellowship within a group of committed believers where they can be totally truthful. I honestly believe the church wouldn't have had the scandals of the late '80s if such a commitment to one another had existed. If ministers had such a fellowship of committed believers where they could "let their hair down" and confess their faults without fear of being condemned, gossiped about, or judged, many of their problems could have been taken care of in private.

I believe the Holy Spirit is going to orchestrate the cooperation between forceful men who will be committed to one another in such a relationship. They will be men who won't try to prove their spirituality, but will instead help one another grow in Christ and in integrity.

Years ago, while I was still pastoring in East Texas, another pastor came to my office to meet with me. He spent a lot of time telling me how he appreciated what we were doing in our church and what I was doing in my ministry.

However, I felt there was something else on the man's mind. When I asked him if there was anything God was dealing with him about, he became flustered and stammered around awhile without really saying anything, and then he left.

Later I found out that this particular minister had been having a problem with pornography. That obsession eventually led to an affair, and today he is out of the ministry. His ministry could have been spared if either of us had understood or been willing to submit to a bond of fraternal fellowship.

2. *Inward character must match outward anointing.*

Perhaps one of the kingdom's greatest disasters is to be a public success and a private failure. People minister under the *anointing*, but they live their daily lives according to their *character*. God is far more interested in character than in exploits.

Oral Roberts says the *anointing* is a divine energy that comes on you, that empties you of yourself and fills you with the presence of God, so when you speak, it is like God speaking, or when you act, it is like God acting.[9]

On the other hand, *character* means faithfulness, integrity, and walking in the fruit of the Spirit. It is a daily, distinctive lifestyle that shows we are good enough stewards to operate in God's provisions to us and to the Body of Christ in any area of life, from finances to ministry.

The two brothers in the parable of the prodigal son in Luke 15 are classic examples. Both received an inheritance. One had faith but no character, whereas the other had character but no faith. In the next move of God, people will have both faith *and* character.

Corrupt character is a slow killer. The gifts and calling of God are without repentance, according to Romans 11:29. It is possible to have a corrupt character and still have God move through you because they are His gifts and callings. Corrupt character, however, is a slow destroyer of the work of God.

A. A. Allen and William Branham are examples of this. One had problems with the flesh and the other with the soul, according to evidence that remains today of their lives.

Allen died of sclerosis of the liver in 1970, reportedly from secret drinking problems. However, miracles still took place in his meetings because of the gifts of God. The ministry eventually eroded and disintegrated because of his character sins. He grew up in a home with an alcoholic parent, and apparently the same problem manifested in his own life.

Toward the end of Branham's ministry, evidence leads us to believe that his prideful desire to stay at the forefront of attention led him into "deep teaching" that ultimately led to actual heresy. His celebrated ministry ended, discredited by his peers. He ultimately got so far off-base that he declared himself, as Dowie had before him, to be the Elijah of God.

3. *Lack of Biblical rest.*

Perhaps the biggest hindrance to the flow of God's Spirit can be found in the lack of rest. In Matthew 11:28, Jesus said, **Come unto me, all ye that labour and are heavy laden, and I will give you rest.** The word *labour* in this context has the connotation of someone underneath a burden, carrying a load. The word *rest* means refreshing, intermission, or break. Jesus was saying an *intermission* would bring a refreshing from things that are burdensome. (v. 29.) *The rest of the Lord* is a coming apart from everyday life for a break in order to hear from God about how to do things according to His ways.

Again, we see in those ministries of an earlier generation that this key of neglecting the need for rest helped bring about downfall. Alexander Dowie sometimes worked as much as forty-three hours at a stretch without rest. Branham so tired himself with long hours of ministry that he required sabbaticals from the pulpit. Welsh revivalist Evan Roberts burned himself out so much in a few years of ministry that he secluded himself for the next forty-five years.

Allen so extended himself in crusades, in television, and in establishing a ministry center and Bible school that his human resources gave out, causing him to reach for chemical help. Other ministers, such as Aimee Semple McPherson, let periodic loneliness and stress provoke ill-timed decisions.

In every temptation, we must learn to go to Jesus and learn His ways; otherwise, we will go back to our old ways. Someone said that we must be like the burning bush — always on fire but never burning out.

How do we remain in God's rest? Everything must be done by God's presence and power. Striving leads to destruction and burnout.

234

Four enemies of staying rested are *overloaded schedules, inadequate sleep, mishandled stress,* and *unchecked sin.*

Learn to say no when the Holy Spirit doesn't say yes to activities. Learn to delegate and give yourself times of relaxation. Get enough sleep and avoid a lifestyle that leads to exhaustion.

To combat stress, learn the principles of joy. The biggest temptation in this area is so subtle that many ministers miss it: They let their schedules cause them to *leave the prayer closet to get things done.* That has arrested many moves of God.

And then, of course, sin will do more to rob a person of rest and peace than anything else. Isaiah said the wicked can't rest and are like a tossing sea. (Isaiah 57:20 NAS.)

4. *Learn prosperity, not materialism.*

As far as I can tell from Scripture, there is only one real reason for wealth, and that is *to establish God's covenant.* (Deuteronomy 8:18.) It isn't wrong to have money, but it's wrong when *money* has *us.* (1 Timothy 6:10.) Seek God, not money.

My advice to young ministers is to decide how much money is enough to live on ahead of time; then when that amount has been obtained, to put the rest back into the kingdom. Money tied up in things not ordained of God is a scheme of the devil to destroy ministries.

5. *Be willing to pay the price.*

This key is not a contradiction to getting enough rest! Jesus Himself told us to count the cost. (Luke 14:28.) We must not assume that any move of God is without cost. Hours of prayer and study of the Word accompany the dynamic flow of miracles. William Seymour often spent five to seven hours in prayer every day prior to Azusa Street. Wigglesworth described *spiritual hunger* as the state where nothing else fascinates you as much as being near God.[10]

We balance *paying the price* with *rest* by first pressing into God and then relaxing. It's like a divine isometric exercise. Press into God; relax. Press into God; relax. That's the only real way to build spiritual muscle.

6. *Bring your family to the same level of faith that you have.*

Your family is a primary attack front for the devil. If he can't get to you directly, he will come indirectly. Countless thousands of ministries have disintegrated because homes were not in order, so make sure you minister to your family before you minister to the masses.

7. *Operate in kingdom laws.*

There isn't enough space in this chapter to outline all of God's kingdom laws, but here is a good example in the area of finances: Aimee Semple McPherson built Angelus Temple *debt-free* during the Great Depression.

Oral Roberts calls it "seed faith." He has used three basic operating principles in his ministry: 1) God is your Source; 2) plant your seed; and 3) expect a miracle. Those three principles invade virtually every aspect of Christian dynamics — whether it is finances, relationships, or ministry.

8. *Fast.*

Fasting was prevalent during past moves of the Spirit, but is virtually absent from today's ministries. Oral Roberts talks of his ministry being birthed in fasting. Jesus' ministry was birthed out of the fasted lifestyle. (Matthew 4:1-11; Luke 4:1-13.) Other ministries of past revivals were founded on fasting. I encourage young ministers to fast one day a week. Fasting doesn't move God, but it does move *us*. Fasting breaks yokes of bondage.

9. *Holiness.*

Wigglesworth once said that there were two things essential for a successful ministry: the *operation of the Holy Spirit* in the meetings and *personal holiness.* We need to see a baptism of holiness in the church again. If God is giving any signal to the church today, it is that He is no longer going to hide His face from sin.

My dad used to say to me when I was growing up, "Son, it's either my way or the highway." And God is saying to His people, "Children, it's either My way or no way."

If any man in history exemplified holiness, Wigglesworth did. He believed that unless a man is holy, pure, and clean, he has no right to expect God to dispense power into his ministry. Wigglesworth's life was an example of the confidence and boldness that holiness alone provides.

I interpret what I have read about his life this way: God can only anoint us in proportion to our truthfulness. We don't need to help the Holy Spirit by our exaggerations. These three things destroy a lifestyle of holiness: fleshly and sexual appetites (lust of the flesh); materialism (lust of the eyes); and the pride of accomplishment (pride of life). Or, as others have said, "sex, money, and power" are the three main temptations of the ministry.

10. *Travailing prayer.*

Every move of God has been preceded by people who have given themselves to prayer. The kind of prayer that often accompanies these moves of God is what some call "travailing" and others call "prevailing." A spirit of travail comes upon people to birth things in the Spirit. Many who have experienced this travail in prayer liken it to giving birth to a baby.

However, *a word of warning:* In recent years, some have fallen into error concerning intercession.

*A spirit of travail* will come upon you as the Holy Spirit wills when you make yourself available for prayer. You can't force it or fake it by making groaning noises in the flesh as if you were "priming a pump." That will either result in soulish prayer, or it will provide access for a false spirit to operate.

Make yourself available to God for prayer; then don't enter into anything other than sincere prayer in English or other tongues without the Holy Spirit moving on you to do so. Some intercessors point out that "birthing" things in the Spirit travails upward, not downward as in the natural order.[11]

The kind of prayer Hannah prayed in 1 Samuel 1 was fervent, and as James 5:16 says, **...The effectual fervent prayer of a righteous man availeth much.** Fervent means "white hot."

The reason that fervent, or travailing, prayer changes things is that it gets us out of the way enough so that we can be completely in tune with, or in agreement with, the Holy Spirit.

These ten areas are keys to the initiation and cessation of the moves of God. The next move will come completely into being when forceful men and women lay hold of the kingdom purely and in line with God's ways. I believe God is raising up a new breed of leaders who will be committed to God, to one another, and to kingdom principles. These men and women will take the world with loving force!

# 11

## *HOW TO MAKE LOVE*

## *TO YOUR WIFE*

*My objective in this chapter is to share with you from a biblical perspective the subject of sex in the Christian marriage. First, I want you to see the heart of God and to hear what God has to say about you making love to your wife. Then I want you to view it from man's perspective.*

*Making love to your wife is not just the act of sex, or sexual intercourse, though that is a part of it. The act of intercourse is one event in the process of making love to your wife.*

**— Creflo A. Dollar, Jr.**

11

## *HOW TO MAKE LOVE TO YOUR WIFE*

by Creflo A. Dollar, Jr.
*Pastor-Founder, World Changers Ministries*
*College Park, Georgia*

I want to talk to you as the leader in your home. You have the responsibility of leading your household and making things work like they should. Being an impacting man of responsibility means to respond and to be able to plot some directions in order to get where you believe God wants your family to be.

My objective in this message is to share with you from a biblical perspective the subject of sex in the Christian marriage. First, I want you to see the heart of God and to hear what God has to say about you making love to your wife. Then I want you to view it from man's perspective.

I'm sure that, before you got born again, you heard sex being presented in street language. You probably heard it while hanging around with the boys in the locker room, or you may have just learned some of these things through discovery.

Making love to your wife is not just the act of sex, or sexual intercourse, though that is a part of it. The act of intercourse is one event in the process of making love to your wife.

### First, as Seen in Proverbs

Let's start in the book of Proverbs, chapter 5, verses 15-19:

**Drink waters out of thine own cistern, and running waters out of thine own well.**

**Let thy fountains be dispersed abroad, and rivers of waters in the streets.**

**Let them be only thine own, and not strangers' with thee.**

**Let thy fountain be blessed: and rejoice with the wife of thy youth.**

**Let her be as the loving hind and pleasant roe; let her breasts satisfy thee at all times; and be thou ravished always with her love.**

Now if you will study the Hebrew text, you will find that the word *fountain* in verse 18 means "body parts which produce life."

Again, in verse 15 it says, **Drink waters out of thine own cistern, and running waters out of thine own well.** The point of this is, if you don't own it, if it isn't yours, then you have no business drinking water from it.

Verse 18 says, **Let thy fountain be blessed: and rejoice with the wife of thy youth.** The word *rejoice* here means to ecstatically delight. This verse is saying, "Ecstatically delight with the wife of thy youth."

Verse 19 is talking about how her love should satisfy him. Notice it says, **...let her breasts satisfy thee at all times.**

Whether you are newly married, are looking forward to being married, or have been married for quite some time, you need to understand what the Bible is saying here. It absolutely, without a shadow of a doubt, makes clear that we as husbands should look forward to a pleasurable, enjoyable and ecstatically delightful experience in making love with our wives.

Some denominations present the picture of a husband and wife never having anything to do with sex until it's time for them to have a baby. But that is wrong. In this Scripture passage, God is simply trying to make a point by saying you should make sure that the waters are your own.

### Now Let's See It From Paul's Perspective

In 1 Corinthians, chapter 7, the apostle Paul says in verse 1:

**Now concerning the things whereof ye wrote unto me: It is good for a man not to touch a woman.**

Notice the word *touch* in this verse. This is obviously not referring to just the general rule of touching, when we go up to somebody and hug or pat that person. Also, Paul is not discussing in this verse the subject of marriage or the wife. When he says a man should not touch a woman, he is talking about touch as the act of intercourse, or intermingling, with a woman. He goes on in verse 2:

**Nevertheless, to avoid fornication, let every man have his own wife....**

He is saying that it isn't good for a man to have sex with any woman other than his wife. He calls that *fornication,* which he says we are to avoid. He is declaring that in order for a man to avoid fornication — to avoid having sex with a woman who isn't legally his, to avoid getting involved with waters that don't belong to him — then every man should have his own wife. He continues in verse 2:

**...and let every woman have her own husband.**

Paul is getting ready to talk about the legal perspective of sexual activity, and he puts it within the confines of marriage, between a husband and his wife. In verse 3 he says:

**Let the husband render unto the wife due benevolence: and likewise also the wife unto the husband.**

This word *benevolence* involves an equality and a respect between husband and wife, especially with regard to having sex. There are times when your wife may not feel like having sex, but she will do it anyway. So, you as the husband will have to render equal respect to your wife and be willing to have sex when she desires it, even when you don't. In other words, don't expect her to do anything that you aren't willing to do yourself.

The Bible goes on in verse 4 to say:

**The wife hath not power of her own body, but the husband....**

Now this doesn't mean you are lord over her body, that you go to her as if wearing a crown on your head and say, "Whether you feel like it or not, you have to make love with me — I'm your husband; you have to submit to me!" Get that kind of talk out of your vocabulary right now.

This Scripture verse says that the wife doesn't have power over her own body, but the husband. Then it says:

**...and likewise also the husband hath not power of his own body, but the wife.**

Because of marriage, his body is no longer just under his own consideration. Someone else has been given a right to his body, and that's his wife. Someone else has been given a right to her body, and that's her husband.

Now remember the objective here. Paul wants to set up an understanding of marriage, so that you will begin to recognize that God is trying to form a oneness between the husband and the wife. He is trying His best to get the man and woman together.

## The Real Challenge Is With the Soul

We know that man is a spirit, that he possesses a soul and that he lives in a body. So the first part of man to be considered is the spirit.

Since 2 Corinthians 6:14 says, **Be ye not unequally yoked together with unbelievers,** we are assuming that these two people are properly married; hopefully, that a born-again man is married to a born-again woman. Their two spirits can then come together. That takes care of the spiritual side of marriage.

The physical part of marriage is dealt with when their two bodies come together in the honeymoon experience.

But the real challenge comes with the part of man, which is the soul. The soul involves the mind, the will, and the emotions. This is where reasoning and logic reside. About two to three weeks into marriage, the husband and wife will find that they have a real challenge to get their two souls hooked together.

This is when they realize that they have different opinions. The husband was raised with one opinion, the wife with another, and they may completely oppose each other. So as they begin to establish their relationship, they become insensitive toward one another, and there will be some clashes.

Now I don't care how "in love" you are in the beginning; the two of you will have these clashes. You might as well just forget about living in Wonderland. In fact, I would dare to say that, after two weeks of marriage, if you haven't already had some type of argument, something is wrong.

When that first argument takes place, your feelings get hurt. After about two or three weeks of marriage, you look at her and say to yourself, *I must have married the wrong woman!* I mean, all of those nice romantic times you were having are spoiled. It had been as if you were living in another world, but then your souls began to clash.

She says something you don't agree with, and it's like a threat to your manhood, especially when she says she isn't going to do what you want. You say, "But I'm the man of this house!" You quickly defend your position and your throne, because you see it being threatened by a rebellious act from that woman. So you pout for a while, saying, "You don't really love me. If you did, you wouldn't talk to me that way."

All of a sudden, life isn't going the way the textbook said it would. The two of you sulk around the house, maybe two or three days, without speaking to one another. Then if you go out in public together, you have to put on a face and look like you both are still so happy.

Don't worry; it's normal for that to happen. And life will still go on. Your marriage will survive as long as, when you got married, you had established the Word of God as your final authority. That's the difference between our marriage as Christians and the marriage of people living the world's way.

So the challenge in marriage is the soul — the mind, the intellect, and emotions. Now the soul and the body bounce off one another, so you have to figure out how to get those two parts together. God had all of this in mind when He developed sex for the Christian marriage. Maybe you have never thought about this before, but the Holy Spirit should be a big part of the sexual relationship you have with your wife.

### Is the Sexual Union Ever To Be Avoided?

Continuing in 1 Corinthians 7, verse 5, it says:

**Defraud ye not one the other, except it be with consent for a time, that ye may give yourselves to fasting**

**and prayer; and come together again, that Satan tempt you not for your incontinency.**

Basically, this is saying, if there is a time in your Christian walk when you don't feel that you should be involved in sexual intercourse, you must remember that your body is not yours; it isn't for you to make that decision by yourself. You have to talk to your wife about it. She will probably want to know why. You will have to explain it to her so that the two of you can be in agreement. It is never just you making your own decision regarding your body; your body doesn't belong just to you.

## God's Promise of Sexual Fulfillment

The promise of sexual fulfillment is available to any husband and wife who will choose to enter into God's plan for their marriage.

Now some people see the sexual relationship in marriage and the pleasure and enjoyment of sex as unholy (and some denominations make people feel that way). Do you see the sexual relationship in marriage as unpleasing? Or, if you are enjoying it, do you feel you ought to be ashamed of yourself? Do you believe that if sex is pleasurable then it is unholy? Do you feel you should be involved in this pleasurable act only to reproduce?

For people who have accepted these inaccurate ideas about the sexual relationship, the result will be a hurried physical act without tenderness or pleasure. A woman who has been married for twenty-five years might never have experienced any sort of sexual fulfillment because the act has not been one of care and concern. It has, instead, been a mechanical act, perhaps the result of religious convictions, but certainly nothing to be enjoyed. There is just no pleasure in sex at all. I mean, who wants to feel like a baby-making machine, whether male or female?

So, you need to understand that you have God's permission to enjoy sex. After all, He invented it. Now let me emphasize that I am talking about this only within the framework of marriage. You don't have God's permission to enjoy sex unless it is between you and your wife, having been joined within the legal frameworks of marriage.

**Therefore shall a man leave his father and his mother, and shall cleave unto his wife: and they shall be one flesh.**

**Genesis 2:24**

What does *cleave* mean? This verse in *The Amplified Bible* and the *New International Version* says they are to be united. In the *New King James Version*, it says they are to be joined. So, to cleave means to stick to like glue!

Notice in this verse it doesn't even talk about being one spirit or one soul; it says they will be one flesh. What is the only way a man can become one flesh with a woman? Through intercourse. Then verse 25 says:

**And they were both naked, the man and his wife, and were not ashamed.**

So God created it, established it and permitted it.

In Mark's gospel, chapter 10, Jesus says:

**But from the beginning of the creation God made them male and female.**

**For this cause** [since God made them male and female] **shall a man leave his father and mother, and cleave to his wife;**

**And they twain shall be one flesh: so then they are no more twain, but one flesh.**

**What therefore God hath joined together, let not man put asunder.**

**Mark 10:6-9**

In other words, it is God Who established this marriage institution and Who established sex in the Christian marriage. Jesus is saying: "Don't let anybody say that this doesn't exist or that it isn't the will of God. Don't let it destroy this institution. God is the One Who instituted sex in the Christian marriage. He knows about sex and He wants to be a part of it within the Christian marriage."

Your sexual relationship with your wife should be getting greater and greater and greater — month by month, year by year.

We find God's expression about marriage again in Ephesians 5:31:

**For this cause shall a man leave his father and mother, and shall be joined unto his wife, and they two shall be one flesh.**

So God is interested in one flesh, isn't He? He is interested in man and woman coming together as husband and wife. God's Word says the marriage bed is holy. Every time God talks about marriage, He is talking about sex. Hebrews 13:4 says:

**Marriage is honourable in all, and the bed undefiled....**

Where is the bed undefiled? Within marriage.

So, what is the reciprocal here? If you have sex when you are not married, then your bed has been defiled. You have defiled the place God had created for sexual activity between the husband and wife. Sex in marriage was not intended just for reproduction; it was intended for pleasure. That means you ought to have pleasure when you experience it. So get rid of the myth that sex is intended just for reproduction.

## Men Need To Understand the Other Side

Now here is another myth, especially in the mind of a man: that it all comes naturally. But that just isn't true.

There are some natural things that happen, but if you want to be a good lover to your wife, there are other things you can do besides the natural things. It is a learning, discovering process.

What a lot of men have done is to lean more towards the discovering process. In other words, they say, "I'm too embarrassed to discuss it." Or "I'm too ashamed to admit I don't know it all." Or "I don't have anybody I can talk to about it. And even if I did, I don't think I would feel comfortable with someone explaining to me about having sex and experiencing love with my wife." Not too many men are really comfortable in this particular setting, because their egos are under attack, as if they were automatically supposed to know all about it.

For the most part, we men were not taken aside early in our lives by our fathers and told all about the area of life which has come to be termed "the birds and the bees." Instead, we got most of our information from the street. What we learned out there was how to fulfill our self-centered pleasures. We didn't hear anything about the other side of the husband-and-wife relationship, which is based on good, satisfying, pleasurable love-making.

So because men haven't heard the other side, they go into marriage with a limited philosophy. This will immediately cause alarms to go off in their marriage because they have never corrected the wrong information they had learned about having sex or making love to their wife.

Now what's the difference between having sex and making love?

Having sex is just the mechanical, self-centered satisfaction a man achieves when he has orgasm. At that moment, he is considering no one but himself. But when making love, he always considers his wife before considering himself. That means the process of making love is

250

not just limited to intercourse; this is something he is doing all of the time, including the time of intercourse.

Many people have been defensive about their knowledge and skill as lovers, feeling that they must pretend to know it all or else have to admit to their personal deficiencies. And that's why I am talking about this area. I don't want you to get defensive over your ego and pretend you know it all. I simply want to deal with you about the process of making love with your wife. Hopefully, through it you will find ways to critique and judge yourself so you can become a better lover to your wife.

## Stages of Making Love

Let's dig right into the process of lovemaking by going through the basic stages involved. We will be looking into things that are very important, things we didn't hear when we were learning about sex on the street.

If you are young and still single, I feel it's important that you learn the right perspective and no longer be subject to wrong ideas. I really believe young men need to learn the right way God intends for them to go when preparing themselves to be the lover to the wife they have chosen for the rest of their lives. Are you ready?

Regarding the process of making love, I want you to realize that it doesn't concern you alone. If you are looking to please only yourself, my brother, you are starting off with the wrong attitude; from the beginning you will be missing it. The act of making love involves not only you, but your wife. It takes two people to tango.

Your objective, your mind-set, should be: *I must please her at all costs.* And it will take some discipline on your part to reach this goal. That's when you will run into this huge area of selfishness — what you find in your life that pleases you.

So, let's lay some ground rules for the process of making love.

## The Setting

First, there is a need for privacy.

You have to understand that a woman's psyche is emotional. She must be completely and totally relaxed. If there is any threat to the emotional part of her, particularly a lack of security when it comes to privacy, then she will never feel comfortable enough to view the experience as enjoyable.

## Lock Your Bedroom Door

So make sure you have a lock on your bedroom door. If you don't have one, get one. In fact, it would be good to have a bedroom and bathroom that are isolated from the rest of your home. Then there would be complete privacy in that area.

If you have children, you need to train them to knock before entering your bedroom. This is very important. It could be an embarrassing or confusing situation, depending upon the age of your child, if he or she quickly opened the door and just came right on in. It can also be really frustrating to the lovemaking process.

My wife and I spent time training our kids to always knock before entering our room when the door was closed and to wait for our response before entering. Anytime they came in without knocking, we made them go back out and do it right.

You have to train your kids from an early age. Even when they knock on your bedroom door, you would want the security of having a lock. Then they can't misunderstand you and say afterward, "Oh, I thought you said, 'Come in.' "

So, put locks on your bedroom door and train your children accordingly. It's important that you provide this feeling of security for your wife. Remember, the part she has to deal with is the emotional psyche.

## Adjust the Lighting

Lighting is important during the sexual encounter.

You need to understand that during lovemaking the husband is greatly stimulated by being able to see his wife's body and by watching her responsive movements and expressions of delight to his actions toward her. So it's good for him when the lights in the room are turned on. But some wives are unable to abandon themselves to the maximum expression of enjoyment by having sex in a room with a lot of light.

Your wife may not necessarily be stimulated by much lighting. She may be somewhat overweight or feel uncomfortable for some other reason. In any case, she just is not satisfied with so much lighting. Often, this can be solved by your expressions of love and appreciation for her. You might want to get a dimmer and set it between darkness and soft lighting. Then you both will satisfy your eyes; and it will satisfy her ability to enjoy herself without feeling all the insecurities that she might feel about her body.

It's important that you get just the right amount of light in the room. If your wife likes more light, then you can make the necessary adjustment. But it is vital that the atmosphere be set up to the satisfaction of both.

Now there are some other things I want to add to having the right atmosphere.

## Make It a Pleasurable Night

This is not really talked about much, but it means a lot to the woman when the man will take the time to shave or shower before making love with her. This communicates to your wife that you feel it important enough to involve yourself in preparation for the big event.

Maybe you are a single man who will be facing the honeymoon experience for the first time after marriage. If you are, you need to recognize that sexual intercourse could be somewhat painful for your new wife (assuming she has never experienced it before). So you both need to talk about different lubrications that can be used to avoid a painful experience on your honeymoon night. It should be a pleasurable night.

It's also important for a man to avoid falling asleep at that time. It would be good for you to have a cold glass of water there on the nightstand to drink. You might also want to keep a couple of towels in the top drawer. You see, at the moment you have completed lovemaking, you might feel like getting up; but that's the time your wife needs to be held and talked to.

You need to concentrate simply on pleasing your wife with tenderness, with romantic words, with warmth, with cuddling, with total body caressing. It should be done in a meaningful way that shows your appreciation of her. She needs to feel that she is a desirable woman to you, and she must be aroused emotionally. That's the key: developing emotional intimacy through physical closeness. Whatever is affecting her emotions will affect that time of intercourse.

Now let's look at "foreplay."

## Foreplay

Foreplay is not just what you do ten or fifteen minutes before actual intercourse takes place. Foreplay is what you do with your wife throughout the entire day — how you treat her, how you care for her, how you communicate with her emotionally. Remember, the most important part about making love to your wife is not intercourse itself, but what happens before and after.

So here are some questions you need to ask yourself: How have I been treating her all along? How do I treat her at times other than sexual intercourse? How do I treat her when she talks to me? How do I treat her when she makes a mistake? Am I spending enough time with her? Am I giving her the assurance she needs every day?

You see, sexual intercourse is a supplement to all of the emotional support you are giving your wife. She is aroused when you say words to her like, "I love you and I appreciate you. You're beautiful to me." When you begin to say such things, they get deposited in the love bank, and she remembers them. You will reinforce this more by what you do for her to make her feel important.

If you are having a rough time in your marriage relationship, when it comes time for intercourse, that's exactly what you will have. But you will miss the anointing of making love to your wife, because you have failed to apologize and to do what's necessary to straighten out all the areas that affect your time of lovemaking together.

So I want you to remember that every conflict you fail to resolve, every area of your marriage relationship you fail to deal with will come back up during your time of intercourse, and it will affect those intimate and meaningful moments.

Now that the lights are low, your tender skills will prepare your wife for the act itself. Most women like to be wooed and won. You should be demonstrating the love you have for her, not just your right to have sex. Don't ever verbalize to your wife concerning your sex rights, saying words like, "I've got a right to it!" That wouldn't be real lovemaking. You would be intensifying her frustration. By doing that, you will have created the ultimate sin: making her feel like an object. She would hate that.

You should be communicating to her that lovemaking is a demonstration of your love for her. Say, "You're so beautiful to me! This isn't a result of my sexual rights; it's a result of my love for you. You mean more to me than all the world." You don't even have to touch her yet. You are getting her ready by demonstrating and communicating your desire to make love to her, by saying: "I love you so much, sweetheart. I want to communicate my love to you, and sexual intercourse is an avenue by which I can do that."

The husband must be careful not to appear hurried or crude or rude, not to appear mechanical or impatient. It isn't what happens in those few minutes when you are trying to set up everything that will communicate your love to your wife; it's what happens hours before sexual intercourse that really tells the story.

You see, if you get hurried, crude and rude and mechanical, in time you will just say, "Oh, forget it; go to bed." You will find that not only will you lose the arousal stage, but she will too. She will say, "You're trying to make this happen too quickly; I need time — don't rush me." You have to be careful not to do that. It will take some discipline on your part, and you will have to make some sacrifices.

Your daily behavior will measure the extent of your sexual pleasure. It's important how you carry yourself every day. That's what good lovers are made of, not what they have in the bedroom but what they do on a daily basis. That's what you have to reexamine.

### Touching

Foreplay also begins with kissing and embracing.

It's interesting to note that after a man and woman have been married for so long, kissing is not a major part of their relationship. But in the beginning, it was a strong part.

It meant so much to him at one time just to have the opportunity to hold her soft hands. Do you remember what that meant to you? Well, try it now. Make it a point to take your wife's hand. Something as small as holding her hand or embracing her with your arm can set up that night perfectly.

When you're in church and the worship of God fills the atmosphere, grab your wife's hand or put your arm around her and begin to worship God together. There is such an ecstasy involved when you're together in the presence of the Holy Spirit. You are loving on God, and your wife is standing right there beside you. Wow! That really is a special experience.

Relaxed love-play in the bedroom begins with kissing, embracing, petting and fondling. In the early part of sex-play, gentle caressing of all the body is the most effective touching for both husband and wife.

Let's say you and your wife are in bed but aren't making love, then she taps you. When she does that, she wants caressing, fondling, embracing. If you take it to mean she is ready for full sex and you move quickly in that direction, you would be ruining the entire moment for her. That isn't what she wants right then.

Now with gentle caressing, embracing and fondling, don't just touch areas that are seemingly related to excitement; touch all areas of her body. Your wife may enjoy caresses on the inner thighs, the lower back, the buttocks, the earlobes. The only way you will be effective in the lovemaking relationship with your wife is for you to find out which she prefers. That won't come by osmosis, it won't just drop out of the air. You have to ask her: "Sweetheart, which areas of your body do you really enjoy for me to caress?"

Now the Bible deals with this subject of touching. In the Song of Solomon 4:7, he says:

**Thou art all fair, my love; there is no spot in thee.**

This was a serious letter. Solomon absolutely had his mind made up. He was saying, "I am satisfied with all of you; there is not a part of you that I am not satisfied with."

Verse 7 AMP says:

**[He exclaimed] O my love, how beautiful you are! There is no flaw in you!**

So, your wife needs to be assured that you are satisfied with all of her.

Of course, there may be some areas in her that you want to identify for correction, such as her need to lose some weight; but right in the middle of making love is just not the time to talk about it. For you to do that would mess up the whole experience. You can talk about it some other time, only in a gentle, loving way. Then you should be committed to assist her in correcting the areas that you have a problem with. It's her responsibility; but since you are the one who has the problem with it, you need to take the initiative to show her ways where you can be a partner with her and assist her in accomplishing what you want done.

When I see my wife's body growing in certain areas, I begin with strong encouragement. I say, "Hey, come on and work out with me today," or "Let's go run together," or "Let's go look for some new diet food." She gets the picture right away.

We husbands must understand that we have a part in that. We just can't throw it off on her. Remember what 1 Corinthians 7:4 says: her body is his, and his body is hers. So we, as husband and wife, need to make some investment in our bodies.

Song of Solomon 5:16 says:

**His mouth is most sweet: yea, he is altogether lovely. This is my beloved, and this is my friend....**

This is what your wife ought to be: your beloved *and* your friend. Verse 16 AMP says:

**His voice and speech are exceedingly sweet; yes, he is altogether lovely [the whole of him delights and is precious]. This is my beloved, and this is my friend....**

You see, it's important for both partners to begin to see one another this same way and to begin to talk. When you see areas of your wife's body that you especially enjoy, tell her. Again, this is emotional arousal.

Tenderness and understanding are key ingredients in the romance that leads up to the intimate relations of marital lovemaking. Men need to know this. But we also need to know some of the actual processes involved in the sex act. As I said, it doesn't happen "naturally." There is a learning process if both husband and wife are to be sexually fulfilled.

So for helpful information on the "how-to's" of the actual sex act, I would like to recommend an excellent book, *Intended for Pleasure*, by Ed and Gay Wheat.* The information contained in it will clear up any misconceptions young or old married couples may have concerning the process involved in the act. And it will teach a healthy perspective and mind-set in regard to the act of sex.

Finally, never forget to take time to express to your wife how you feel. Say from your heart, I love you very much. Hug her often. Tell her how much she means to you. Do little things for her. These are all important aspects of making love to your wife. Let her know that she is special and that she is attractive to you.

---

* Ed Wheat, M.D. and Gay Wheat, *Intended for Pleasure* (Grand Rapids: Fleming H. Revell, 1977).

If there are areas you need to repent of and to ask her forgiveness for, then do that right away. It really isn't important who is at fault. There should be reconciliation at all costs. You are to be married to her forever.

And always remember that learning how to make love to your wife is an on-going process which is never fully learned. Each new day has new opportunities to grow in your relationship. So pray for the Holy Spirit's help in being sensitive to your wife's special needs. Ask Him to teach and guide you in those times of gender confusion when you want to laugh, but she wants to cry. Or when you want to "channel cruise," and she wants to talk. And never forget that the act of intercourse is only one aspect of making love to your wife.

# ENDNOTES

[1]Peck, Scott M. *The Road Less Traveled*. (New York: Simon and Schuster, 1978).

[2]Lindsay, Gordon. *John Alexander Dowie* (Dallas: Christ for the Nations, Reprint 1980).

[3]Woodworth-Etter, Maria. *A Diary of Signs & Wonders* (Tulsa: Harrison House, Third Printing, Copyright © 1916 by M. B. W. Etter).

[4]Valdez, A. C. *Fire on Azusa Street* (Costa Mesa: Gift Publications, 1980).

[5]Liardon, Roberts. Video Lecture Series, "God's Generals" (Tulsa: Infinity, 1988).

[6]Lindsay, Gordon. *Adventures in God* (Tulsa: Harrison House, 1981).

[7]Harrell Jr., David Edwin. *All Things Are Possible* (Bloomington: Indiana University Press, 1978), p. 25.

[8]Montgomery, G. H. "The Enemies of the Cross," *International Healing Magazine*, pp. 140-144.

[9]*Holy Bible, Oral Roberts Personal Commentary, New Testament Section* (Tulsa: Oral Roberts Evangelistic Association, 1981), p. 41.

[10]Hibbert, Albert. *Smith Wigglesworth* (Tulsa: Harrison House, 1982), p. 27.

[11]DePastino, Dr. Valerie. *Endtime Commissions, Endtime Anointings* (Tulsa: Christian Publishing Services, Copyright © 1988 by Dr. Valerie S. DePastino).

# OTHER SOURCES AND RECOMMENDED READING:

1. Evans, Eifion. *The Welsh Revival of 1904*. Wales: Evangelical Press of Wales. Copyright © 1969 by the Evangelical Movement of Wales.

2. Lindsay, Gordon. *The John G. Lake Sermons*. Dallas: Christ for the Nations. Copyright © 1949 by Gordon Lindsay. Reprinted 1986.

3. Pratney, Winkie. *Revival*. Springdale: Whitaker House. Copyright © 1983 by Winkie Pratney.

# ABOUT TIM STOREY

Tim Storey is a strong leader in the Body of Christ today. His unique motivational style of speaking followed by Christ's miraculous signs and wonders is changing the lives of thousands around the world.

Tim also ministers on a monthly basis to many of Hollywood's "stars." His down-to-earth presentation of Jesus is bringing hope to many in the entertainment industry.

*Maximum Impact*
is available from
your local bookstore
or by writing:

**HARRISON HOUSE**
P. O. Box 35035
Tulsa, Oklahoma 74153

To contact Tim Storey,
write:

Tim Storey Ministries
1421 E. Firestone, Ste. 303
La Mirada, California 90638

*Please include your prayer requests
and comments when you write.*

In Canada contact:
Word Alive
P. O. Box 670
Niverville, Manitoba
CANADA ROE 1 EO

**The Harrison House Vision**

Proclaiming the truth and the power
Of the Gospel of Jesus Christ
With excellence;

Challenging Christians to
Live victoriously,
Grow spiritually,
Know God intimately.